Judy DuCharme

# THE CHEESEHEAD DEVOTIONAL

Daily Devotions for Packer Fans

## Hall of Fame Edition

**SonRise Devotionals**
Lighthouse Publishing of the Carolinas

THE CHEESEHEAD DEVOTIONAL: HALL OF FAME EDITION BY
JUDY DUCHARME
Published by SonRise Devotionals
an imprint of Lighthouse Publishing of the Carolinas
2333 Barton Oaks Dr., Raleigh, NC 27614

ISBN: 978-1-946016-33-1
Copyright © 2017 by Judy DuCharme
Cover Design: Elaina Lee
Interior design by Karthick Srinivasan

Brought to you by the creative team at Lighthouse Publishing of the
Carolinas: Cindy Sproles, Shonda Savage, Denise Loock, Elaina Lee, and
Karthick Srinivasan

Library of Congress Cataloging-in-Publication Data
DuCharme, Judy.
The Cheesehead Devotional: Hall of Fame Edition/ Judy DuCharme 1st ed.

Printed in the United States of America

# Praise for
# The Cheesehead Devotional
# Hall of Fame Edition

As a man of faith and with a profound interest in the Green Bay Packers, I can tell you that the two are joined seamlessly in Judy DuCharme's *The Cheesehead Devotional: Hall of Fame Edition*. The motivational words that accompany each Packer story are impactful, each serving as a compass for all walks of life, for all ages of fans. And within every challenge are a lesson to be learned and an avenue toward hope.

This book is a blessing to comfort you when it's fourth and one, or you've just fumbled in your own life. With Judy's stories of the Packer greats, your playbook is filled with inspiration and verse to take you to a win in the greatest game of all.

~ **Kevin Harlan**
CBS, TNT, Westwood One Sports
and son of Bob Harlan

Judy has truly depicted each Hall of Famer's everyday norm into a wonderful parallel of our daily lives from the "Playbook." The reading is simple, the characters are very different, Coach Lombardi's challenge will guide us one day at a time, and last, don't forget your extra point that day … it is a freebie. We all love free stuff, and this freedom is given to everyone who will accept it.

~ **Sara White**
Wife of the late Reggie White

Judy does a great job of combining real life and real faith with personal football experiences, specifically Packer football. "God, Family, and the Packers" is not just a saying; it is a way of life. *The Cheesehead Devotional: Hall of Fame Edition* will help all Christians live out their faith daily.

~ **Steve "The Owner" Tate**

We consider the Packers on Sunday in the fall a religion in Wisconsin. Judy DuCharme has taken the quotes of Lombardi and the spirit of some of the greatest Packer players of all time and skillfully woven them into a series of inspirational messages for us all.

~ **Wayne Larrivee**
Game-day radio voice of the Packers

*The Cheesehead Devotional: Hall of Fame Edition* is an astounding book compiled with faith and trust. From a fan's perspective, Judy DuCharme portrays amazing reverence for not just the players but also for the Green Bay Packers organization. Judy brings forth pure charisma of character with the sincerest respect for the players. This allegiance is inspirational and heartwarming.

~ **Wayne D. Sargent**
The Ultimate Packer Fan
ultimatepackerfan.com

# Table of Contents

*I dedicate this Hall of Fame Edition of* The Cheesehead Devotional *to Packer fans far and near, young and old, who have loved their team and supported it in loss and victory. This book can never tell all that each Hall of Famer has done, but it touches on a few aspects, some well known and some not so well known, and draws a truth from each life that can bless and direct our own. May each reader enjoy this journey into the history, commitment, and excitement of the Packer Hall of Famers and be blessed and encouraged to live life as God purposed.*

# Foreword

Life is a mysterious journey. When we come into this world, we do not have the opportunity to foresee what is in store for us. For some people, the road is rosy and great, but for others it is rocky with many obstacles.

Unfortunately, mine has taken the rocky road. I am a cradle Catholic as are my four children. They were raised having to attend church. As they got older, they chose their own paths and drifted along the way. Eventually, though, they realized, *Hey, I really do need this religion thing and God in my life.* I allowed them to fly with their own wings—there is not much else you can do but nag, and that has no purpose. It has to be in their hearts.

I have had to deal with a lot of adversity, pain, embarrassment, and misfortune. Many other families have and will experience similar situations. Unfortunately, because of Brett's fame and success, everything that happens in our family is national news.

My friends and family know I live one day at a time. Making plans does not usually fly in my life. My strange journey began at age 10 and has continued through the years. People have asked me why I am not in Whitfield (our state mental institution). I just look up to the heavens and point.

My Lord and Savior has walked the walk with me and has given me the strength to continue down my path of life. Besides the woes, there have also been great memories, success, and love!

I have depended on many devotional books and the word of the Lord. I feel like Judy DuCharme's new devotional book is just what I need to continue this journey. I commend you, Judy, on all your effort and work and wish you great success.

**~ Bonita Favre**
Brett's Mom

# Life That Excites

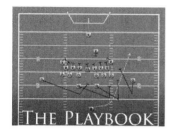

**FROM THE PLAYBOOK:**

*A merry heart does good, like medicine, but a broken spirit dries the bones.*

Proverbs 17:22

**COACH'S CHALLENGE:**

"If you aren't fired with enthusiasm, you will be fired with enthusiasm." Vince Lombardi

Driving through Green Bay, I glanced at the car next to me. The car was big, but what caught my attention was the driver's resemblance to Antonio Freeman, wide receiver for the Green Bay Packers. I looked again to be certain. I saw the proof in the big grin he gave, and then he blew me a kiss. Made my day.

The Packers certainly hold celebrity status in the Green Bay area, but most residents take it in stride and don't bother the players for autographs and pictures. We love to see them around town and say hi. Many of us consider them family, neighbors, good friends.

Antonio Freeman is well known for one of the greatest ever Monday Night Football plays. I attended that game. However, he considers his greatest play a catch in Super Bowl

XXXI against the New England Patriots.[1] The ball was deep in Packer territory at the beginning of the second quarter. Quarterback Brett Favre dropped back and launched the ball from the 13-yard line. Freeman caught it on the Packers' 45 and ran untouched 55 yards into the end zone, securing a lead we never gave up. Freeman lobbed the ball over the goal posts and did a celebratory dance.[2]

Freeman was a happy player. He enjoyed the game, enjoyed his role, loved catching the ball and scoring. You might say, "Hey, who wouldn't?" Yet, you've seen the players who get in fights during the games, arrogantly taunt opposing players, or pout when they don't get the ball. They fume when a penalty is called on them . . . or not called on the other guy. Sometimes we feel scrappy along with them, especially if it looks like we're going to lose or the call seems unfair. But Freeman, like Brett, enjoyed the game and kept it in perspective. He chose to live a life that excites and to get excited when he played well.

Our lives can be lived that way too. It may only take a momentary adjustment . . . sometimes several times a day.

Do you ever think God wants us to live a life that excites, to have a faith that excites? Can you imagine having a faith that excites God? Imagine God saying to the angels, "Now, that guy right there impresses me. I like watching him."

Not going to happen with you?

Well, consider if you've ever said that about your child or if your parent said that about you. Perhaps you've said that about a student or an employee. What made that person exciting? They went out of their way to accomplish something, took risks, and had fun along the way.

It's possible for all of us to live in that exciting way . . . with a momentary adjustment . . . sometimes several times a day. Definitely possible.

**EXTRA POINT:**

Dear Lord, I'm making a wild little adjustment today to be exciting to You in the choices I make and the things I do. Help me to please You.

*Antonio Freeman, Wide Receiver, Inducted into the Packers Hall of Fame 2009*

# Checking the Numbers

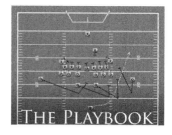

**FROM THE PLAYBOOK:**

*So teach us to number our days, that we may gain a heart of wisdom.*

Psalm 90:12

**COACH'S CHALLENGE:**

"Truth is knowing that your character is shaped by your everyday choices." Vince Lombardi

"Jesus is coming. Are you ready?" Reggie White asked the opposing player as they lined up at the line of scrimmage. Players and fans considered it Reggie's means to intimidate, but often he was only taking the opportunity to find out if the player knew the Lord.

While playing with the Philadelphia Eagles before he came to Green Bay, Reggie kept asking that question of a Detroit Lions' lineman who cursed him every time they lined up against each other. At one point, just before the ball was snapped, Reggie snarled, "Here comes Jesus!" With a single shove on that play, he sent the man back five yards. Whenever Buddy Ryan, the coach, needed a big play from Reggie, he'd yell, "Get out there and tell 'em Jesus is coming!"[3]

For six seasons, we loved to chant "Reggie! Reggie!" in

Lambeau Field and watch him burst through an offensive line with his swatting club move and wrap up the quarterback in an amazing sack. He attained 198 sacks before his retirement from the NFL.[4] His three sacks of Patriots' quarterback Drew Bledsoe helped the Packers win Super Bowl XXXI. When I met Reggie, he seemed twice my height and three times as wide. He was huge. And kind. And a man of God.

Reggie had no problem reconciling Christianity and football. He eagerly stood on the nationwide platform that professional football provided and shared his faith. Known as the Minister of Defense, he prayed for teammates and led both teams in prayer after every game.

The Packers retired Reggie's number 92 as did the Philadelphia Eagles, where he spent seven seasons. The University of Tennessee, his alma mater, also retired his number 92.[5]

Reggie knew to number his days. Perhaps he had a sense that his life would be cut short. He died of a deadly combination of sarcoidosis and sleep apnea when only 43. Perhaps he determined to not miss a single moment of life sharing the love of Jesus, enjoying the goodness of God, and seeking to obey Him in all he felt called to do.

What does "number our days" mean to you? We often think the instruction is to be wise about how we spend our time, to not waste it. That, indeed, is good advice. In the Hebrew, the word conveys a deeper meaning: to appoint. Make each day an appointment to fulfill God's calling, to hear His voice, to pay attention to what's important. More than not wasting the day, it means to make the day count, to mark it for good. Pay attention to those around you.

Do what is right. Do what is necessary. Direct the day to accomplish the plans and purposes God has placed within you. Enjoy each day, knowing God is guiding you.

**EXTRA POINT:**

Lord, I will appoint my days for good, for Your blessing, in obedience to You. I choose now to make my daily life count for Your purposes.

*Reggie White, Defensive End, Inducted into the Packers Hall of Fame 2006*

# Arise and Shine

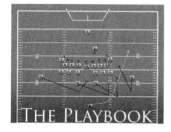

THE PLAYBOOK

**FROM THE PLAYBOOK:**

*Do not rejoice over me, my enemy; when I fall, I will arise; when I sit in darkness, the Lord will be a light to me.*

Micah 7:8

**COACH'S CHALLENGE:**

"It's not whether you get knocked down, it's whether you get up." Vince Lombardi

"He'll be fine. Get back to work!" Lombardi just found out his steel coaching tower blew over due to a strong gust of wind and landed on linebacker Ray Nitschke. A bolt from the tower pierced Nitschke's helmet, stopping just shy of his skull and only inches above his left temple. Most of the players removed their helmets moments before the tower fell. Nitschke put his back on due to the rain, not wanting to get his head wet. His teammates freed him from the tower, and they all went back to practice.[6]

Ray's nickname was "Animal." His roommate said, "He was like a raving madman on the field and a teddy bear off of it."[7] This was Nitschke, number 66, one of the greatest and most fearsome NFL middle linebackers of all time.

Ray's father died when he was three, and his mother died when he was ten. Football provided the means for him to take out his anger. However, because of his loss, he extended compassion to others in need and was extremely generous off the field.[8]

Players and coaches considered Ray a tenacious tackling machine. But he could do much more. In October of '67, he picked off a Lions' pass and ran it 20 yards for a Packers' touchdown, increasing the lead to 20-10. He accumulated 25 interceptions in his career.[9]

At Ray's funeral in March of 1998, John Bankert, director of the NFL Hall of Fame, told those gathered, "I first met Ray Nitschke about 20 years ago. When I shook his hand, he scared the heck out of me. I last saw him about two months ago. I shook his hand, and he still scared the heck out of me."[10]

"He could put the fear of God into people," Bart Starr said of him. Later in life, after coming to know the Lord, Nitschke desired to share the love of God with everyone.[11]

Ray got knocked down many times. And he got back up as well. On the playing field, he often rose with a negative, vindictive attitude, but in life, he learned to get back up with an attitude to help others. He exhibited kindness and recognized kindness in others. When a local pastor spent time with Ray and his wife before her death, Ray responded to that kindness and prayed to know the Lord.

Tough times can make us mean and resentful, or we can allow those tough times to build in us a resolve to be kind and generous to others. Dependence on the Lord will help us make that choice. If life has been rough for you, consider choosing to make the lives of others easier.

**EXTRA POINT:**

Thank You, Lord, that I'm tough enough to always be kind.

*Ray Nitschke, Linebacker, Inducted into the Packers Hall of Fame 1978*

# Run to Win

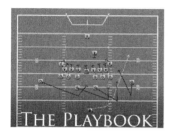

THE PLAYBOOK

**FROM THE PLAYBOOK:**

*Do you not know that those who run in a race all run, but one receives the prize? Run in such a way that you may obtain it.*

1 Corinthians 9:24

**COACH'S CHALLENGE:**

"Only one team is going to win this. Run to win!" Vince Lombardi

The summer of '67 was brutal for the Packers. None of the players knew how brutal the championship game against Dallas would be. But Coach Lombardi seemed to know. He demanded every ounce of their energy every day. "This is the big push. It starts now." He said it every few days all season long.[12]

The morning of the Ice Bowl, the championship game against Dallas, dawned at 13 degrees below zero. "No gloves!" barked Lombardi. The wind chill at the beginning of the game was minus 41 degrees. Bart Starr fumbled the ball on the first play. The ref blew the whistle, and the metal froze to his lip. He pulled it off, tearing his lip. The blood oozed and froze. No more whistles sounded; instead, the refs yelled "Stop!" at the end of each play.

By halftime, the field crusted over, which made the footing terrible. Dallas took the lead 17-14 in the fourth quarter, having sacked Bart Starr eight times. Jerry Kramer reminded the team of the July training camp, the exhausting time when they gave their all, when Lombardi instilled in them "run to win" and taught them pride, courage, and determination. This was the day for which that training prepared them.[13]

Sixteen seconds remained on the clock. Third down with no time-outs on the one-yard line. Starr called a 31 Wedge. The center snapped the ball, and Kramer burst off the line. Remembering "run to win," he pushed Jethro Pugh, Dallas front lineman, out of the way. Instead of giving the ball to Chuck Mercein, protocol for 31 Wedge, Starr kept it and executed one of the greatest quarterback sneaks of all time. The Packers won 21-17 and moved on to play in Super Bowl II.[14]

Has your year been brutal? Have you wanted to quit? Has someone pounded you with demands to do more, give more? Has God called you to do something, to win a race in an area of your life? Does the call seem unrelenting, the work unending, the atmosphere so cold you feel you can't perform?

Remember that whom God calls, He equips. His strength enables you to accomplish great works. He tells us, "all things are possible" (Mark 9:23), and "we are His workmanship" (Ephesians 2:10). Isaiah 40:29 tells us that He gives strength to the weak and increases the strength of those who have no might. The key is to wait on the Lord. Instead of hashing it out and venting with friends, let that happen with God. Grab that five minutes or 50 minutes alone with God. Take time to listen and be strengthened. Then go out and "run to win."

**EXTRA POINT:**

Lord, I thank You that I can run the race set before me as long as I keep my eyes on You.

*Bart Starr, Quarterback, Inducted into the Packers Hall of Fame 1977*

# Welcome Home

**FROM THE PLAYBOOK:**

*But now in Christ Jesus you who once were far off have been brought near by the blood of Christ.*

Ephesians 2:13

**COACH'S CHALLENGE:**

"I firmly believe that any man's finest hour, the greatest fulfillment of all that he holds dear, is that moment when he has worked his heart out in a good cause and lies exhausted on the field of battle—victorious." Vince Lombardi

The favorite son was home again. I stood in Lambeau Field July 18, 2015, as Brett Favre walked out the tunnel amidst the deafening five-minute standing ovation. The cheering crowd, 67,000 strong, welcomed him back to the place known as his kingdom for sixteen seasons. Brett's eyes filled with tears as he said, "If there were any doubts before, there's not any now."

Like the prodigal son, he felt unsure if he would be welcomed back. Some fans had crossed him off years before. Others never did. Either way, that day all was forgiven, and once more Brett belonged to us, the Packer nation.

"Playing at Lambeau Field, running out of the tunnel . . . there's nothing like it on this earth. I've also run out of that [visitor] tunnel, and that was scary." Brett played against the Green Bay Packers when he was a Minnesota Viking . . . a distasteful event to Packer fans. At this homecoming, however, we reclaimed our ownership of Brett Favre as one of the greatest quarterbacks in all of football. He was home and inducted into the Packer Hall of Fame. Not only that, but we retired his number 4 at the same time. No one else would wear that number except for all the fans who still love to wear the Favre jersey.

Second chances. Restoration. God is so big on that. And so were the Packer fans. When Brett spoke about his induction into the Hall of Fame, he said out of all those he needed to thank there was "none more important than God. My faith has gotten stronger as I've gotten older."[15]

As time goes by, are you bigger on second chances and restoration like God is? Do you fear you might be unwelcomed by God, as Brett wondered if Packer fans would reject him? Not one person in the world is ineligible for God's forgiveness and restoration. Jesus came to seek and save the lost.

Can you extend a second chance to others who've offended you? Want to be like God? Forgive and restore. Want to know God? Accept His forgiveness and restoration.

**EXTRA POINT:**

Dear Lord, I commit myself to extend forgiveness and second chances to all those around me, as I receive it for myself from You, my amazing God.

*Brett Favre, Quarterback, Inducted into the Packers Hall of Fame 2015*

# Let Miracles Rule

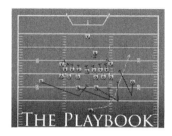

**FROM THE PLAYBOOK:**

*Jesus Christ is the same, yesterday, today, forever.*

Hebrews 13:8

**COACH'S CHALLENGE:**

"Success is like anything worthwhile. It has a price. You have to pay the price to win and you have to pay the price to get to the point where success is possible. Most important, you must pay the price to stay there." Vince Lombardi

"I haven't ruled out a miracle." Ken Ruettgers wanted to play in the Monday night game against the Bears. He'd prayed with so many others when God performed a healing miracle for Reggie White the previous year. Reggie's hamstring injury almost kept him out of an important game, but God was greater.

Two weeks before the Bears' game, Ken played against Washington in the last pre-season game of the 1995 season. Shortly before the half, the Packers executed a running play into the end zone. Ken twisted in his block, and stretching when he stood, he dropped immediately to the ground. He thought he'd been kicked in the back. Instead, four small bones in his spine cracked, a result of his contortion in the tackle and pileup. Still in great pain, Ken sat out the first game of the regular season against the Saints but provided towels, drinks, and encouragement to his teammates. Without Ken at left tackle, quarterback Brett Favre sustained numerous hits, and the Packers lost to the Saints 17-14.

Ken hoped to play in the next game against Chicago, and he believed God could accelerate the healing process. When speculating reporters and hopeful fans asked him if he'd play, he gave two answers. "I'll see if I can put my shoes on first," and "I haven't ruled out a miracle." Not only did Ken Ruettgers play in the Monday night game, but he also played pain free without any medication. The Packers won 27-24.

Pepper Burress, the Packers' trainer, said the healing was mystifying—accomplished by God, not the trainers. Burress totally understood the extent of the injury, the pain, the protocol, and the usual pattern of recovery. In his mind, Ken's recovery was a miracle.[16]

Do you hesitate to trust God when you're in a difficult situation? "Why would He do it for me?" is a question that plagues many. Another person's blessing may deflate our hope. We convince ourselves that others did something significant, didn't do something detrimental, or are more special in God's eyes. We don't always see the walk of faith that helped them overcome obstacles of doubt and questioning. We see the end result—favor, healing, success.

What if we looked at that end result in other people's lives and said, "I'm next. If God did it for them, He'll do it for me. I'll persevere in prayer and belief. God is no respecter of persons, and their faith, their battles, their successes are stepping stones for me." Wouldn't that attitude give us more to rejoice about and less to complain about?

**EXTRA POINT:**

Dear Lord, I will place myself in line for a blessing from You.

*Ken Ruettgers, Tackle, Inducted into the Packers Hall of Fame 2014*

# The Landry Trophy?

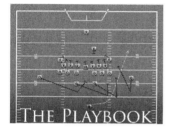

THE PLAYBOOK

**FROM THE PLAYBOOK:**

*There are diversities of gifts, but the same Spirit. There are differences of ministries, but the same Lord. And there are diversities of activities, but it is the same God who works all in all.*

1 Corinthians 12: 4-6

**COACH'S CHALLENGE:**

"The achievements of an organization are the results of the combined effort of each individual." Vince Lombardi

The team liked singing. Lombardi liked singing. He figured if a player sang in front of his teammates, he demonstrated courage. And more than anything else, Lombardi liked courage.

After the Packers won the 1966 Western Conference championship game against Baltimore, the flight home rang with singing. Fuzzy Thurston, starting left guard for eight seasons, got it going, as usual. He belted out, "He's got the whole world in His hands." Then he sang, "He's got the greatest quarterback in His hands," followed by "the greatest coach." Everyone joined in and considered it the best-ever flight home after a game.

The singing and fun provided much-needed relief for Lombardi since the pressure was on. He was expected to win—for the good of the league. It wouldn't look good if the Packers lost. Lombardi was indomitable, but he seemed anxious about this one. Still the team trusted him. At times, a few players hated him, but he'd trained them well. He didn't allow for effort to be anything less than 110 percent.[17] Thurston kept the spirits up. His motto was "never, never quit." Lombardi leaned on him.

That flight home encouraged them all. Their next task required beating the Dallas Cowboys so the Packers could play in the first Super Bowl. Who knew what an iconic game it would be? Lombardi knew Dallas studied the Packers' every move as they prepared to stop his team, so he reversed every play.

His plan worked—for part of the first quarter. The Packers were up 14-0. Dallas caught on and came back. By the end of the first quarter, the score stood at 14-14. Anger and frustration filled the Packer defense. Thurston came to the sideline and said, "Hey, don't worry about it. We'll get it back. Don't worry about it."[18]

The Packers kept pressing, and late in the fourth quarter, we led 34-27. However, Dallas was on our two-yard line.

In the huddle, Willie Davis, defense captain, said, "This is it. This is it." He told his teammates if they didn't get it done, they'd carry regrets forever.

With 45 seconds left, Dallas quarterback Don Meredith took the ball at the two-yard line and rolled to the right. The Packers' left linebacker, Dave Robinson, burst through the line and chased Meredith as he tried to set his feet and throw. Robinson wrapped him up as Meredith released the ball. The ball hurtled toward the center of the end zone, and Tom Brown, right safety for the Packers, grabbed the ball for the interception and the win.[19]

Bill Curry, Packers' center, speculated that if Coach Tom Landry's Cowboys had completed that pass and won the game, then gone on to win Super Bowl I, perhaps the Lombardi trophy would be the Landry trophy.[20] That thought alone sends shivers through Packer fans. We take great joy in the ownership of the Lombardi trophy. The true home of the Lombardi Trophy is Lambeau Field, but one play could have changed that.

One play can set the course for your life. One decision can affect the future of a team, a family, a business. The Packer players' decisions were group-agreed-upon decisions, but they were also individual decisions followed by effort. We often don't see or realize the effect of decisions and efforts until we look back. However, hindsight can set the stage for future efforts and decisions.

Will you do your part, play your game to the best of your ability, remembering that someday you'll look back and realize that one choice or one action made the difference in your life or someone else's life and future?

**EXTRA POINT:**

Dear Lord, I will set my heart and mind to make good choices followed by effort so that one day I can look back with joy.

*Fred "Fuzzy" Thurston, Guard, Inducted into the Packers Hall of Fame 1975*

# Players Become Fans

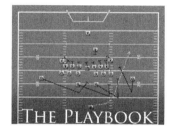

**FROM THE PLAYBOOK:**

*From whom the whole body, joined and knit together by what every joint supplies, according to the effective working by which every part does its share, causes growth of the body for the edifying of itself in love.*

Ephesians 4:16

**COACH'S CHALLENGE:**

"Teamwork is what the Green Bay Packers were all about. They didn't do it for individual glory. They did it because they loved one another." Vince Lombardi

"Heck yes we screamed. A 53-yard field goal? Man, I was high-fivin' with my good arm." Edgar Bennett was pumped despite the pain. Earlier in the October 1996 game with the 49ers, after a much-disputed Packer touchdown, Brett Favre threw to Edgar Bennett for a two-point conversion. Bennett landed on his shoulder. The injury forced him to leave the game, but his play brought the score to 17-14 49ers. Bennett joined Brooks, who'd suffered a knee injury on the Packers' first drive of the game, and Dotson, who'd sprained his left ankle early in the third quarter.

Bennett bringing the score to within three points of the 49ers helped turn around a difficult game. For the rest of the game, the three injured players watched, cheered, and prayed from a treatment table in the locker room.

Chris Jacke tied the game with a 35-yard field goal. The locker-room trio cheered. Then Favre threw an interception. Groans went up in the locker room. With 1:50 left in regulation, 49ers' Coach George Seifert passed on the opportunity to take a shot at the end zone from the 10-yard line. Playing it safe, he took a 20-17 lead with a field goal. Favre scrambled to the 13 with only 30 seconds left and no time-outs. The injured trio yelled, "Win the game! Skip the field goal! Win the game!" Three pass attempts to the end zone proved unfruitful. Jacke's 31-yard kick sent the game to overtime. The trio cheered anyway.

Holmgren decided to go for a 53-yard field goal to win the game. Bennett and Brooks held their breath. Dotson put his head between his knees. Hugs and high fives followed the win.[21]

Bennett, Brooks, and Dotson weren't thinking about their pain but about the team. Everything within them wanted to be on the field, but they rooted together for a win. Proverbs 17:22 says that laughter does good like medicine. For these injured Packers, winning did the same good. Their recovery took time, but their devotion to the team and desire to win never wavered.

Can you root for your team when you're unable to participate? Too often we gripe and complain when we can't play in the game, or we may decide that our replacement will not do as good a job as we would. How much better to see the big picture, forget our momentary setback, and remember who we are—a part of something much bigger. The family of God can be victorious in this culture. We need to simply remember we're each a member of the body and then do all we can to support each other.

**EXTRA POINT:**

Dear Lord, I will walk in the knowledge that I'm a member of the body of Christ. I will contribute and assist others so the body can function at its fullest.

*Edgar Bennett, Running Back, Inducted into the Packers Hall of Fame 2005*

# Replay the Majik

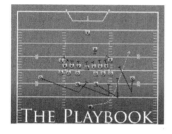

THE PLAYBOOK

**FROM THE PLAYBOOK:**

*To You, O my Strength, I will sing praises; for God is my defense, my God of mercy.*

Psalm 59:17

**COACH'S CHALLENGE:**

"The real glory is being knocked to your knees and then coming back. That's real glory. That's the essence of it." Vince Lombardi

Fourth and goal at the Bears' 14-yard line. Thirty-two seconds left in Lambeau. A cold November 5 in 1989. Four seasons since the Packers last beat the Bears. Humiliating. Quarterback Don Majkowski threw a touchdown pass to wide receiver Sterling Sharpe to tie the game 13-13. Deafening cheers, then silence. A referee threw a flag. Majkowski had stepped over the line of scrimmage. The touchdown would not count.

However, this was the first season of instant replay. The play was reviewed for four minutes while 56,500 fans waited. Some held their breath as Bill Parkinson, instant replay official, studied the footage and conversed with the other officials. Many fans stood, giving the touchdown signal—sure the touchdown counted. If the penalty held, it would cause the loss of down, returning the ball to the Bears. The game would end 13-7 Bears.

The announcement came. The refs reversed the call and the touchdown held! Some worried that the stadium wouldn't withstand the stomping, jumping, and cheering. Chris Jacke kicked the extra point and won the game, 14-13.[22]

After the game, linebacker Brian Noble said he'd never been in favor of instant replay, "but what was that guy's name? I've got to send him a bottle of champagne or something."[23]

Known as the Majik Man, due to an easy mispronunciation of his last name, Don Majkowski became the great hope of the Green Bay Packers. His smooth, calm style provided him the ability to find second and third receivers. He came in second behind Joe Montana in 1989 for MVP. That year, he had over 4,300 yards passing with 27 touchdowns, accumulating the second-highest totals in Packer history. In early 1992, he reinjured his ankle, a problem that plagues him to this day. In came a young, undisciplined, wildly successful Brett Favre. Sterling Sharpe said of the Majik Man: "Had he been able to stay healthy, you may have never heard of Brett Favre."[24]

Challenges and reviews abound in our lives, in our jobs, in our families. Don Majkowski and the Packers believed the best while the officials reviewed the famous play. Stepping over the line of scrimmage would've been so easy as he dodged tackles and waited for receivers to get open. This was the last play, the last chance to win the game. He made the play, but because of a possible misstep, the touchdown was taken away. Due to the review, it was given back.

It's hard to turn crucial decisions over to those who hold the power to give and take away. But it's wise to put our lives, our every step, every moment, in the hands of the Judge of all Eternity. His judgment will stand even when the world cries foul. He sees all; He knows all. As we learn to hear and obey His voice within us, we'll find that official reviews in our lives will support the truth.

**EXTRA POINT:**

Lord, I choose to let You be my guide and judge and to live my life to the fullest for You.

*Don Majkowski, Quarterback, Inducted into the Packers Hall of Fame 2005*

# Giving It All

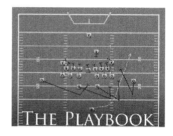

THE PLAYBOOK

**FROM THE PLAYBOOK:**

*But I discipline my body and bring it into subjection lest when I have preached to others, I myself should become disqualified.*

1 Corinthians 9:27

**COACH'S CHALLENGE:**

"The man on top of the mountain didn't fall there." Vince Lombardi

He'd rather run over you than go around you. Jim Taylor consistently looked for a safety to run over before he looked for a hole to run through. And he seemed to gain energy from everyone he hit.

The Packers hailed the 1962 championship game against the New York Giants as the coldest game the players had ever played. Throwing the ball was not feasible. At 18 degrees and plummeting, the winds raged 25 to 40 miles an hour. Number 31, Jim Taylor, ran the ball 31 times, gaining 85 yards. During the first quarter, Sam Huff, Giants' linebacker, hit Taylor hard in the helmet, causing him to bite his tongue. He swallowed blood the rest of the half. The impact also gashed his elbow. At halftime, a doctor stitched him up, and he continued to play. The Giants went after him the whole game, kneeing and pounding him into the freezing ground. Huff said he did everything he could to Taylor, but Taylor simply looked at him, spit, and asked, "That your best shot?"[25]

When Taylor arrived in Green Bay in 1958, he didn't look big enough or fast enough to last in the NFL, but he became the all-time rusher for the Packers from the 1960s until 2009 when Ahman Green broke his record. Taylor had five straight 1,000-yard seasons. In 1962, he was the NFL Player of the Year with 1,474 yards. Taylor loved playing "knockdown, hard-knock football." He loved contact. He told reporters, "You know you'll be subject to pain and suffering. You just accept it. It's combat. You accept it up front."

For nine seasons, Taylor gave the team his all, submitting his body to a beating every week. The symbol of power in the Packer attack for so many years continued to enjoy excellent health with no aches and pains even past the age of 80. He jogged five to six miles each day, lifted weights, and did push-ups.[26]

Giving our all to a cause, a job, or a purpose doesn't mean we'll suffer for it the rest of our lives. Jim Taylor is a great example of this. Of course, he did his part to stay fit and strong. Many times we hesitate to submit to a calling, assuming it'll be too exhausting, too demanding, too difficult. Yet the Bible gives us the principle of sowing and reaping. Jim Taylor sowed physical commitment and reaped health.

Can you trust God enough to commit to the preparation and the effort necessary for what He wants you to do? Can you follow up that effort with the trust that you'll continue in strength after you've completed that calling?

**Extra Point:**

Lord, I commit my life to preparation and effort so I can complete the calling You've given me. I trust You to guide me into a healthy and long life.

*Jim Taylor, Fullback, Inducted into the Packers Hall of Fame 1975*

# Go for It!

THE PLAYBOOK

**FROM THE PLAYBOOK:**

*For what man knows the things of a man except the spirit of the man which is in him? Even so no one knows the things of God except the Spirit of God. Now we have received, not the spirit of the world, but the Spirit who is from God, that we might know the things that have been freely given to us by God.*

1 Corinthians 2:11-12

**COACH'S CHALLENGE:**

"The harder you work, the harder it is to surrender." Vince Lombardi

Chris Jacke hit the 53-yard field goal to win the game in overtime. The 49ers were livid. An earlier touchdown that could have been disallowed turned the momentum. Behind 17-6 in the third quarter, Brett Favre threw a pass to Donald Beebe, in for the injured Robert Brooks. Beebe landed on the ground and cradled the ball as Marcus Pope dove for him. Beebe then popped up, unaware of a possible

touch from Pope. He ran another 29 yards to obtain the
TD. Replays showed that Pope may have grazed Beebe and
that the ball may have touched the ground. Nevertheless,
the touchdown was upheld. Bennett ran for a two-point
conversion, bringing the score to 17-14.[27]

In that game, Jacke kicked four field goals in regulation—a
30-yarder and a 25-yarder in the first quarter along with a
35- and a 31-yarder in the fourth quarter. The last one sailed
between the goal posts with 1:42 left on the clock, tying the
game. Coach Holmgren had declined sending Jacke out for
a 51-yard attempt earlier in the game, thinking his defense
could get the ball back. But in overtime, fourth and five,
with more than 11 minutes left, Holmgren decided to try
it. A miss could set the 49ers up for the winning field goal.
Holmgren didn't hesitate; he went for it.

The 49ers were a formidable team in the 1990s. That
Monday night battle was one of the biggest games of the
season. Craig Hentrich set the ball and said he knew Jacke
had it. "I could tell right away." Still, it was a gamble. Jacke
had missed important kicks that year. He was 16 of 25 over
50 yards but hadn't attempted any that season. The kick was
good, making the final score 23-20. The Packers' record
moved to 6-1.[28]

Taking a risk is indeed that—risky. We can't foresee the
outcome. If it works, we praise the person's wisdom. If it
doesn't work, we disdain the reckless action. When the Holy
Spirit dwells within us, we gain an internal advocate. Over
time, He trains us to know His ways so we can rely on our gut
instinct. When faced with split-second decisions, we often
rely on past experience, logical projection, greatest need, or
a gut feeling. Decisions that are necessary and unexpected

often require immediate choices. There may be nothing in our experience or training that gives us a sense of what to do. Everything we know may tell us to go one way, but our gut tells us to go another direction.

Many will tell you that going with their gut was the right decision. You can increase the percentage of good choices by allowing the Holy Spirit to lead you daily in big and small decisions. Practice going with your spirit—your inner man, your gut—in small decisions, when life does not depend on it. That will build your sensitivity to the Spirit and improve your ability to recognize good decisions. Feed your spirit with prayer and Bible study so you can sense what truly comes from the Lord. As a coach and a player over time know what's needed and go with it, you'll become confident with the important decisions in your life.

**Extra Point:**

Holy Spirit, You are welcome in my life. I give You freedom to direct and train me so I make excellent choices, big and small.

*Chris Jacke, Kicker, Inducted into the Packers Hall of Fame 2013*

# The Gift of Leadership

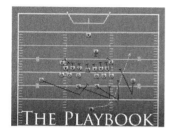

THE PLAYBOOK

**FROM THE PLAYBOOK:**

*Unless the Lord builds the house,*
*they labor in vain who build it.*

Psalm 127:1

**COACH'S CHALLENGE:**

"Leadership is based on a spiritual quality—the power to inspire, the power to inspire others to follow." Vince Lombardi

"Judy, Just a quick note to thank you for *The Cheesehead Devotional.* I love it—and I know our fans will as well. Thanks again, Sincerely, Mark Murphy."

How cool is that! Much to my surprise and delight, Mark Murphy sent a handwritten thank-you note for the copy of *The Cheesehead Devotional: Kickoff Edition* I left for him at Lambeau Field. Others have told me that the president of the Packers often handwrites letters to fans. Imagine the time involved. And imagine the goodwill. It thrilled me as I totally did not expect it.

A few months later, my phone rang. Bob Harlan's voice greeted me, returning my call. Really? I had recently conversed with his son Kevin at a gathering and told him

I'd love to give his dad a copy of *The Cheesehead Devotional.* Kevin told me to call his dad to get the address. When I got his answering machine at his Door County home, I figured I wouldn't hear from him. Instead, he called me back and said he'd love a copy. After we chatted, I sent him the book. He sent me a thank-you note, which I promptly framed, just as I had the note from Mark Murphy. Kindness from someone so well known often seems a surprise.

Why do we suppose that someone who has great success or power won't be kind, won't take time for the common people? Those who work hard to gain success are often willing to help someone else do the same. Bob Harlan is such a person, and so is Mark Murphy.

Harlan started with the Packers in 1971 as assistant general manager. He is credited with the redevelopment of Lambeau Field, which increased the stadium's capacity from about 61,000 to over 72,500. As a result, the additional Packer revenue moved the team from the bottom third of the league to the top third. Harlan said, "God tapped us on the shoulder and told us it was time to go with this."[29]

During his tenure as Corporate General Manager, Assistant to the President, Executive Vice President, President and CEO, and Chairman of the Board, Harlan answered his own phone at the office. Some calls were pleasant, and some were not. Still, he took the job himself rather than giving it to a secretary. "I think since these people own this team, if they want to reach me, they should be able to do so."[30]

Hiring Ron Wolf as general manager in 1991 is considered Harlan's crowning achievement as president of the Packers.

Wolf hired Mike Holmgren; he also signed Brett Favre and Reggie White. Wolf said of Harlan, "He did exactly what he promised. He put me in charge of the football operations and never once did he interfere." Ron Wolf's philosophy was to use the draft and develop the young players into the players needed by the team. He had the patience to mold them, to identify what needed to be corrected, and then to make corrections.[31]

Harlan hired Ted Thompson in 2005.[32] Mark Murphy became President and CEO in January 2008 as Harlan retired. He expanded Lambeau Field, led in the community development of the Titletown District, improved the infrastructure of the Packer organization, and added a Super Bowl to the Packer legacy. "He gets it as far as the relationship between the fans and the team and how important the team is to Green Bay and Northeastern Wisconsin," said Thomas Olson, lead director of the Packers.[33]

People who know how to manage well are quite impressive. People who know how to trust the Lord as they manage are even more impressive. And people who are kind to people as they manage are the most impressive. Let's never lose sight of the Lord and everyday people as we work on fulfilling our dreams.

**EXTRA POINT:**

Dear Lord, may I always be ready to assist those who seek to follow in my footsteps.

*Bob Harlan, President, Inducted into the Packers Hall of Fame 2004*

*Ron Wolf, General Manager, Inducted into the Packers Hall of Fame 2000*

# Hit Hard and Speak Kindly

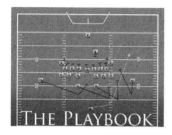

**FROM THE PLAYBOOK:**

*For he who would love life and see good days, let him refrain his tongue from evil, and his lips from speaking deceit.*

1 Peter 3:10

**COACH'S CHALLENGE:**

"You never win a game unless you beat the man in front of you. You've got to win the war with the man in front of you. You've got to get your man." Vince Lombardi

"Get to the Bronk before he gets to me." Clarke Hinkle stated his plan simply when it came to Chicago Bears' tackle Bronk Nagurski. Thirty pounds heavier and a formidable opponent in 1934, Nagurski trapped Hinkle near the sidelines and knocked him back five yards. Hinkle lowered his shoulder as he was hit and broke Nagurski's nose and one of his ribs. At a game in Chicago, Nagurski hit Hinkle so hard that he had to be carried to a hospital for three stitches, but he returned to play in the fourth quarter. As a college player for Bucknell University, Hinkle was known as the Bucknell Battering Ram. Though a running back, he could pass, punt, catch, kick, and tackle.[34]

When Hinkle entered the Pro Hall of Fame in 1964, Nagurski gave the induction speech.

Can you be best friends with your strongest opponent? Are you able to enjoy the company of someone who has bashed you in front of the world? Football players often heat up on the playing field and get into fights. However, the great players can compliment each other in the tension of the battle. They recognize and strategize how to defeat the other player without hating him.

That's a tall order, but what a sign of great character. Each of us needs to perform our calling and position to the best of our ability. In doing so, we may upstage someone, but at times we'll be upstaged by another person as well. Acknowledging the triumphs of others while still doing our best to be victorious is a path to excellence and satisfaction in our job and purpose.

Hinkle didn't always win against Nagurski, but at the enshrinement ceremony, Hinkle simply said, "Bronko, I am proud to sit in the Hall of Fame with you. Today I feel like the boy who has climbed the highest tree in the woods and conquered the forest. What else is there?"[35]

Life is full when you do your best. What are you doing today?

**EXTRA POINT:**

Lord, thank You for helping me to do my best, to be victorious, and to honor those who are victorious over me.

*Clarke Hinkle, Running Back, Inducted into the Packers Hall of Fame 1972*

# Where's Your Identity?

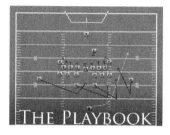

**FROM THE PLAYBOOK:**

*For He made Him who knew no sin to be sin for us, that we might become the righteousness of God in Him.*

2 Corinthians 5:21

**COACH'S CHALLENGE:**

"Once a man has made a commitment to a way of life, he puts the greatest strength in the world behind him. It's something we call heart power. Once a man has made this commitment, nothing will stop him short of success." Vince Lombardi

Tony Canadeo stood one inch from the goal line and threw a touchdown pass to Don Hutson. When Coach Lambeau scolded him for passing so close to the goal line, Canadeo responded, "Cecil Isbell tossed a four-incher not long ago for a record and I wanted to beat it—you don't get an opportunity like that very often."[36]

Halfback, and sometimes quarterback, Canadeo was the all-time leading rusher at his retirement. To this day, only Jim Taylor, Ahman Green, and John Brockington are ahead of him. He backed up quarterback Cecil Isbell in 1942, passing for 310 yards, rushing for 272, and throwing three touchdown passes.

Joining the Packers in 1941, Canadeo retired in 1952 along with his number 3—only the second number to be retired by the Green Bay Packers.

So how did the kicker for the Packers receive that retired number in 1961? Ben Agajanian, an amazing kicker, played only three games with the Packers, but they mistakenly gave Canadeo's number to him. Agajanian had lost four toes on his kicking foot in a work accident and wore a squared-off shoe. His great kicking helped the Packers win a championship.[37]

Imagine Canadeo's reaction when he saw 3 on the kicker. Imagine the kicker's chagrin, or perhaps pride, knowing he wore Canadeo's retired number.

Canadeo became tougher when he put on number 3. His teammate and good friend Tom Miller said, "When he put that uniform on, he changed. He was tough and ready to go all the time." Lee Remmel, Packer historian, praised Canadeo's ability. "He could do just about anything. He was a good runner, a good blocker, a good returner, and a good receiver. He was one of the toughest players the Packers ever had."[38] I wonder if Agajanian, a great player in his own right, felt different with Canadeo's number on his back.

When we take on an identity, especially another person's identity, life changes. Jesus took on the uniform of man and submitted to death followed by resurrection. He wore our uniform so we can wear His uniform—His life and covering. In Isaiah 61:3, the Bible says we've been given the garment of praise for the spirit of heaviness, the oil of joy for mourning, and beauty for ashes. We exchange our bad for His good. When we take His identity, we receive life, strength, joy, peace, and provision. When we put on Jesus' uniform, we'll be tough and ready to handle life, just like Canadeo and Agajanian with number 3.

**EXTRA POINT:**

Lord, I receive the covering—the uniform of Your identity—so I can walk in Your strength through every situation I face every day.

*Tony Canadeo, Running Back, Inducted into the Packers Hall of Fame 1973*

# Blessed Confidence

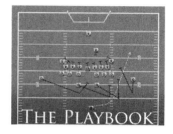

**FROM THE PLAYBOOK:**

*And whatever you do, do it heartily, as to the Lord and not to men.*

Colossians 3:23

**COACH'S CHALLENGE:**

"We would accomplish many more things if we did not think of them as impossible." Vince Lombardi

The first play of his first game with the Packers, Brett Favre audibled a play the team hadn't practiced, and the Bengals immediately sacked him. Brett fumbled four more times in the game. Mike Holmgren in his first year as a head coach said to himself, "I'm never gonna win a game in this league."[39] The Packers, in their third game of the 1992 season, already stood at 0-2. First-string quarterback Don Majkowski tore an ankle ligament in the first quarter, and second-string QB Ty Detmer was also hurt. The game against the Cincinnati Bengals rested on Favre.

The fourth quarter opened 17-3 Bengals. Terrell Buckley gave the Packers a touchdown with a 58-yard punt return. The Bengals answered by scoring a field goal. The next possession, Favre connected with Sidney and then scrambled 20 yards himself. Cheers rose several decibels. Sterling Sharpe caught a pass for 30 yards, bringing the Packers to the seven-yard line. Bennett ran the ball to the five. Seconds later, Favre hit Sharpe again to bring the score to 20-17 with 4:11 left on the clock. The announcer said Favre had strength but "no touch."[40] Could this untested gunslinger secure a win?

Buckley fumbled the next punt return. The Bengals moved into field goal range but kicked wide right. A false start gave them a five-yard penalty and a second opportunity. The Bengals scored the 41-yard field goal.

Nineteen seconds left. Packers down by six points. Favre moved the ball from the eight-yard line to the Bengals' 35. Kitrick Taylor came in to replace Sharpe. Sharpe suffered bruised ribs on the earlier touchdown, left the game, came back in, reinjured himself, and went out again.

Head Coach Mike Holmgren called an all-go. All receivers ran straight down the field. Brett dropped back to the 40, pump-faked, and pushed a blocker out of the way. He then turned right and fired a wild high-arching pass down the field to Taylor. Collective groans and gasps filled Packer land. Taylor couldn't possibly catch that crazy pass. But he did! And he scored the tying touchdown. Despite missing two field goals earlier in the game, Chris Jacke kicked the extra point to seal the win.[41]

We listened to the game in the car on the way home from church. Our son kept saying, "Mom, stop pounding the dashboard!" But the excitement engulfed me. We watched the game again 20 years later while we vacationed in Florida. Our son put in the DVD as we prepared to enjoy the dazzlingly beautiful 78-degree day in March. Although we knew the Packers won the game, we couldn't remember how, so sitting on the end of the bed, glued to the TV, we bled green and gold. We even argued as to whether the retry of the Bengals' field goal resulted from a defensive or offensive penalty. We reentered the emotion of the game.

The excitement and tension of a come-from-behind win are always high. Emotions connect to every play, and the win or loss is keenly felt. The Bible teaches us that the end of time is at hand. Emotion, tension, and excitement fill the air in all realms of life. The Bible also makes it clear that our Lord wins; we're members of the triumphant team.

The Lord isn't an untested gunslinger like Favre in his first game, or like we may be in many areas of life. Imagine the determination and all-out effort in that young man as he took the reins. We can have the same confidence, not in our ability, but in the ability of the one who gave His life for us and promises to give us victory every day. With God in us, so much is possible. Trust Him, and even with only 19 seconds left, you can do it.

**EXTRA POINT:**

Lord, I thank You that through Your strength I can do everything You designed me to do.

*Brett Favre, Quarterback, Inducted into the Packers Hall of Fame 2015*

# Seeing Beyond

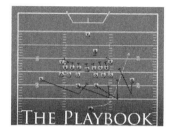

**FROM THE PLAYBOOK:**

*While we do not look at the things which are seen, but at the things which are not seen. For the things which are seen are temporary, but the things which are not seen are eternal.*

2 Corinthians 4:18

**COACH'S CHALLENGE:**

"After all the cheers have died down and the stadium is empty, after the headlines have been written, and after you are back in the quiet of your room and the championship ring has been placed on the dresser and after all the pomp and fanfare have faded, the enduring thing that is left is the dedication to doing with our lives the very best we can to make the world a better place in which to live." Vince Lombardi

Although well known for not talking to the media while he remained in Green Bay, Sterling Sharpe gave one memorable radio interview. Steve Rose hosted a Packer show with Ken Ruettgers. Without telling Steve, Ken secured Sterling's agreement to visit the show—maybe the only radio interview Sterling Sharpe ever gave in Green Bay. He shared that a newspaper had misquoted him his first season, so he shut down his contact with the media. He came to Green Bay to play football well, so he decided to focus only on that.

Sharpe met his goal to play well. He led the NFL in receptions three of those years and in receiving touchdowns for two seasons. He started every game of his career and attained All-Pro five times. When Steve asked Sterling if he thought he could deal with a season-ending injury, he replied, "Yeah, I think so. If God would have my career come to an end, I believe that I could deal with that." The interview was just weeks before the neck injury that ended Sterling's career. In one game, a block snapped his head back, and in the next game, a tackle aggravated the injury. The two hits created an abnormal loosening of the first two vertebrae, and doctors highly recommended that Sharpe quit playing immediately. He did.

In the interview with Rose, Sterling talked about his growing relationship with God and how much he enjoyed the Packer Bible Accountability Group that met weekly for the Christians on the team.[42]

A little-known fact about Sterling Sharpe is that despite his refusal to sign autographs publicly or talk to the media, he came into the team locker room on his day off to read boxes of letters requesting his autograph. He sat in front of his locker and signed them all.[43] Today he's a sports analyst, a part of the media.

Although many fans loved Sharpe as a player, they didn't like his refusal to interact with them. In fact, other players, coaches, and the Packer administration often found him exasperating. In spite of all that, he played superb football, came to know the Lord, and signed autographs in private.

Every person is unique. We can be so quick to judge another person by actions that don't seem right. The Bible instructs us in Romans 14:4 to not judge another man's servant: "To his own master he stands or falls. Indeed, he will be made to stand, for God is able to make him stand."

Can you look beyond another's actions even if, by all rights, that person is wrong? It's a strong challenge. It's the type of thing that God requires of good character. He sets a high bar for each of us in daily life.

**EXTRA POINT:**

Lord, help me to look beyond the actions of others and to believe and pray for the favor of God upon them.

*Sterling Sharpe, Wide Receiver, Inducted into the Packers Hall of Fame 2002*

# First One

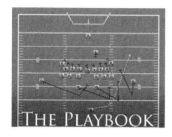

**FROM THE PLAYBOOK:**

*Furthermore, we have had human fathers who corrected us, and we paid them respect. Shall we not much more readily be in subjection to the father of spirits and live?*

Hebrews 12:9

**COACH'S CHALLENGE:**

"I've never known a man worth his salt who, in the long run, deep down in his heart, didn't appreciate the grind, the discipline." Vince Lombardi

What a debut! The Chicago Bears had their eye on Johnny Blood in that 1934 game, not on rookie wide receiver Don Hutson. Blood's incredible speed as a running back and a receiver had already helped lead the Packers to three consecutive NFL championships.[44] The Packers won the toss and returned the kick-off to their own 17-yard line. Blood lined up right of quarterback Arnie Herber while the rookie Hutson, in his first game with the Packers, lined up left. Blood went down the right sideline, taking some of Chicago's secondary with him. Herber dodged some hits before firing deep to the left. The rookie collected the pass on the Bears' 43-yard line and flew untouched into the end zone. That was the first of 99 touchdown receptions in a career that lasted eleven seasons and brought Hutson accolades of being one of the greatest receivers, not just for the Packers but for the whole NFL. No one broke his record of most career touchdown receptions until 1989.[45]

Johnny Blood was born John Victor McNally but took the name Johnny Blood for his entire professional career and signed all his contracts Johnny Blood.[46] Eccentric and flamboyant, he became known for his antics off the field. He loved hard work and would occasionally "ship-out to the Orient as an ordinary seaman and enjoy the beauty of the Pacific Islands" in the off-season.[47]

Herber grew up in Green Bay and sold programs at the games as a young man. He played football at Green Bay West High School and the University of Wisconsin and then worked as a handyman for the Packers. That career ended the day Coach Curly Lambeau gave him a try-out. Former teammate Harold Van Every said he had the "greatest arm I've ever seen. The man was a terrific passer." Herber and Hutson became the league's first dynamic quarterback-receiver pair.[48]

Don Hutson's number 14 was the first number to be retired by the Packers in 1951. He was considered the genesis of the modern receiver. Most games were pounded out on the ground in the 1930s. Coach Curly Lambeau made a change to emphasize the aerial approach, and Hutson created many of the routes currently used in the NFL, such as buttonhooks, hook-and-gos, and Z-outs.[49] Hutson also played kicker and safety. Upon retirement, he held 18 records, 10 of which still stood at his death in 1997.

In his amazing career with the Packers, Hutson, a man of commitment and creativity, demonstrated the vital importance of focused practice. The Packers named their newly built indoor practice facility The Don Hutson Center three years before he died. The practice facility provides a place for current and future Packers to work and acquire Hutson's versatility and focus.

Often we have no idea what our example will be to those who follow. When we do our best, we aren't necessarily thinking about whom we might influence. You may not be written about in years to come. You may not set records for others to admire, emulate, and attempt to break. You may not realize that the tweaks and ideas you introduce in your line of work may affect your field for years to come. However, when you set out each morning with passion for whatever you are called to do that day, your legacy can positively influence all who follow.

Versatility, commitment, and creativity are admirable values, especially when walked out each day. Daily football practices may be dull, fatiguing, and painful at times. The dailiness of life is often that way no matter what we're engaged in. Realizing that we can create, set records, and improve the system is the challenge to keep in the back of our minds and at the forefront of our purpose.

**EXTRA POINT:**

Lord, my best is in Your hands, and I'll allow You to shape me and what I do as You see fit.

*Don Hutson, End/Defensive Back, Inducted into the Packers Hall of Fame 1972*

*Arnie Heber, Quarterback, Inducted into the Packers Hall of Fame 1972*

*Johnny Blood (John McNally), Running Back, Inducted into the Packers Hall of Fame 1970*

# Eyes to See

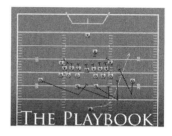

**FROM THE PLAYBOOK:**

*May He grant you according to your heart's desire, and fulfill all your purpose.*

Psalm 20:4

**COACH'S CHALLENGE:**

"It's about the will to win and to endure, and preparation is the only way you can do this." Vince Lombardi

Willie Davis considered it one of the team's best-ever defensive stands, and he always knew Dave Robinson would be the one to analyze and execute the necessary play. Five minutes remained in the fourth quarter of the 1966 championship game against Dallas. The winner would play in Super Bowl I. Tom Brown, Packer backup safety, had blown a play, allowing Cowboys' tight end Frank Clarke to score. The Packers still led 34-27. Their next possession, however, was a three-and-out. With a little over two minutes left on the clock, Dallas possessed the ball on the Packer 47-yard line. Quarterback "Dandy" Don Meredith and Clarke went after Brown again. Brown anticipated the play but guessed the wrong direction for Clarke. He grabbed the tight end, resulting in a pass interference call that moved the Cowboys to the two-yard line.

The Cowboys reached the one-yard line on first down. A false start on second down backed them up to the six-yard line. Meredith tossed a quick swing pass to Reeves, who dropped the ball. When the third down pass fell short, the Cowboys were back on the two-yard line. One play left.

The Packer defense said little before the play. They knew what they had to do. The ball was snapped to Meredith, and Dave Robinson saw an opening. It wasn't his lane or where he was supposed to be, but Robinson knew how to improvise. He and Willie Davis planned and strategized every single game. Robinson pushed through that hole, forcing Meredith out of the pocket. All he could do was heave the ball into the end zone and watch a herd of Packers and Cowboys grapple for it. Tom Brown, the safety who'd allowed a touchdown and received the pass interference call, got that ball.[50] The Packers won because they kept playing, despite mistakes, improvising where needed. Redemption belonged to Tom Brown because Dave Robinson analyzed quickly and improvised with great skill.

Davis said, "Dave was a huge playmaker, someone we could trust to get the job done when the game was on the line." He spent his time examining every detail of his opponent's play and studying all the variations he could.[51]

Improvisation succeeds when we're thoroughly prepared. A seed in its container or in our hand doesn't grow. But when planted in soil, it germinates, sends out roots, receives nutrition, and grows according to the great design it holds within.

Dave Robinson planted the plays and strategies of

football within himself. Because the game germinated in him, he perceived the possibilities and ramifications, and great abilities came forth when needed. It's the same with the Word of God, the Bible. Just carrying it around or saying we believe it accomplishes very little, but when we immerse ourselves in God's Word, fill our hearts and minds with His truths, and study to know His ways, we'll be quick to sense His promptings. Then, when we're in the midst of life's important decisions, it will appear we improvise well because we've taken time to know God, absorb His words, and learn His ways.

**EXTRA POINT:**

Dear Lord, I commit to take the time to prepare my heart with Your truths and Your ways so I'll make wise decisions.

*Dave Robinson, Linebacker, Inducted into the Packers Hall of Fame 1982*

# He Touched Downs
# and More

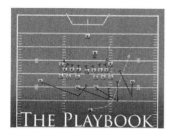

**FROM THE PLAYBOOK:**

*But Jesus called them to Him and said, "Let the little children come to Me, and do not forbid them, for of such is the kingdom of heaven."*

Luke 18:16

**COACH'S CHALLENGE:**

"Don't succumb to excuses. Go back to the job of making the corrections and forming the habits that will make your goal possible." Vince Lombardi

"I always thought the first Super Bowl was the most significant event in my life, but it wasn't. The most significant moment in my life was when my son was diagnosed with diabetes." Max McGee, the iconic voice of Packers' football for 20 years has stories and humor galore. Every Packer fan knows the story of Max partying all night before the first Super Bowl because he knew he wouldn't play. As a backup, he'd only participated in a few plays all season. Then Boyd Dowler injured his ankle and McGee came in. Almost immediately, he caught a Bart Starr pass with one hand—

slightly behind him, no gloves—and ran it in for the first Super Bowl touchdown. He didn't even have his own helmet on. And he went on to score five more touchdowns. Many thought he should have received the Most Valuable Player award rather than Bart Starr.[52]

McGee spent eleven seasons with the Packers. He married early in his career and had two daughters. Later, he and his wife divorced. Remarrying at age 51, he had two sons, Maxie and Dallas. Maxie, born with Down syndrome, became his dad's constant companion. Dallas was diagnosed early in his life with diabetes, and Max founded the Max McGee National Research Center for Juvenile Diabetes in 1999. He's raised millions of dollars for the Center with his annual golf tournaments and speaking engagements.[53]

The field of professional sports provides a giant platform and opens doors to incredible possibilities, but the issues of life often steer us where we never intended to go. My son was also born with Down syndrome. After the shock, after the devastation, after the adjustments to daily life with changes you never planned on, you find new determinations, passions, and sensitivities. Depression may attempt to hold you back, but the choice to go forward, to find the best, and to work for betterment will be the wisest direction.

Max McGee was "one of the most talented natural athletes we had," according to Paul Hornung. Max enjoyed tremendous success in sports, the restaurant business, and broadcasting, but what he felt defined him was helping his boys and others afflicted with similar diagnoses.[54]

Do your circumstances shape you? Do you allow them to point you toward the positive or the negative? Our lives overflow with varied seasons, many talents, and a host of possible ventures. When we look back on our lives, what we did for others will define us. Are you allowing God to direct you into ventures that will bless others? Will you be known for what you contributed to other people's lives?

**EXTRA POINT:**

Lord, I thank You that I am more than my talents and business ventures; I am more than what people remember about me; I am what I do for others and especially for You.

*Max McGee, End, Inducted into the Packers Hall of Fame 1975*

# The Grave Digger

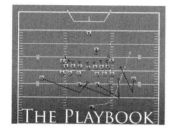

**FROM THE PLAYBOOK:**

*Having disarmed principalities and powers, He made a public spectacle of them, triumphing over them in it.*

Colossians 2:15

**COACH'S CHALLENGE:**

"The spirit, the will to win and the will to excel—these are the things that will endure and these are the qualities that are so much more important than any of the events themselves." Vince Lombardi

Every fan delighted to see Gilbert Brown dig an imaginary grave after a monstrous tackle. A big man, Brown knew and enjoyed his expertise at nose tackle for the Green Bay Packers. After plowing into one or two opposing players, wrapping them up, or landing on them with his bulk, he popped up, stuck one leg out, and skipped on the other one as he pretended to dig with a shovel. The crowds loved it. They loved Gilbert. One local burger place even named a triple-decker burger the Gilbert Burger.[55]

Number 93 enjoyed the accolades, but he placed priority on doing his job so others could do theirs. "That tackle position right there, you have to be unselfish because you really have to do a lot of things in order for everybody to have a good game."[56] During the 1996 season, the one in which the Packers won Super Bowl XXXI, Brown had 51 tackles. In each game, he lined up next to Santana Dotson, Sean Jones, and Reggie White.[57]

Before a big game in San Francisco, Reggie pulled the team into a meeting room to show them film of the 49ers and point out their weaknesses. Gilbert related how Reggie convinced them that the 49ers weren't invincible. With the confidence Reggie gave them, the team went to San Francisco and beat the 49ers soundly.[58] At the Super Bowl, when it came to the fourth quarter and the game needed to be sealed, Gilbert tackled his man, freeing up Reggie to sack Drew Bledsoe three times. The Lombardi Trophy came back to Green Bay.

Gilbert superbly executed his position and showed his pleasure by digging the imaginary grave. Our Lord defeated the Enemy of our souls and put him in the grave so we could do the dance of victory. Because Jesus died and rose again, I don't have to dig a grave. Instead, I can rejoice even before my victory comes.

Unlike football, where the players are unsure of victory, the Bible assures me that in Christ Jesus I'll always triumph (2 Corinthians 2:14). I can rejoice ahead of time, not arrogantly but confidently, knowing all things will work out for my good and God's purpose. Jesus put the Enemy in the pit and made a show of him openly. I can delight in that.

**Extra Point:**

Thank You, Lord, that I can rejoice right now for the victories still in front of me.

*Gilbert Brown, Defensive Tackle, Inducted into the Packers Hall of Fame 2008*

# Off-ense or Of-fense?

**FROM THE PLAYBOOK:**

*Looking carefully lest anyone fall short of the grace of God; lest any root of bitterness springing up cause trouble, and by this many become defiled.*

Hebrews 12:15

**COACH'S CHALLENGE:**

"Winning is habit. Unfortunately, so is losing." Vince Lombardi

Warren Sapp blindsided Chad Clifton. Sapp called the play necessary. Coach Mike Sherman called it a cheap shot.

Tampa trailed Green Bay 7-6 in the third quarter on November 24, 2002, at Raymond James Stadium. Cornerback Brian Kelly picked off Brett Favre and ran 31 yards. Left tackle Clifton gave chase from 20 yards away. He couldn't catch Kelly. But someone caught him.

Players always focus on the ball, either to advance it or stop it. The moment an interception occurs, offense becomes defense and defense becomes offense. Sapp said when his defensive team switches to offense, he's required to make a block. Otherwise, he'll get called out when the team has film playback. He looked for the quarterback, but Favre wisely trotted off the field. He aimed next for the left tackle, Clifton. Sapp crossed the field and struck him right below his facemask. Clifton dropped hard to the ground and stayed there 15 minutes while staff worked on him. The medical staff loaded him onto a stretcher, and an ambulance transported him to the hospital. He remained there four days as a result of damage to two bones of his pelvis joint and ligament tears.[59]

Clifton's season ended that day. Weeks passed before he could walk without assistance. He required six months of rehab in order to begin the 2003 season. Amazingly, he started all 16 games. The league determined Sapp's hit to be legal. However, three years later the league reversed its standing and placed a penalty on anyone hitting a defenseless player. Years later, Clifton remarked, "I wish it hadn't happened but, hey, it's football."[60]

Early on, Clifton hoped for an apology but made the choice to let it go. He didn't take offense. If initially offended, he didn't hold on to it. Many Packer fans held that offense longer, and I joined them. The replays showed the hit was unnecessary even though it was expected behavior after a pick. And the seriousness of the injury could easily have ended Clifton's career, not only his season. Sapp seemed to carry an arrogant attitude about it, so I found it easy to hold a grudge.

Grudges come easy. Forgiveness, not so much. The Bible tells us in Hebrews 12:15 that a root of bitterness can defile, or mess up, many. Have you noticed that? If you allow an offense to sink deep and take root, it colors so many things. It's not pretty. Soon you're offensive to and affecting others with your bitterness. Forgiveness doesn't deny the act or the results, but it is your free card out of jail—the jail of your own making, full of torturous thoughts and heaviness. I needed to choose to forgive Sapp too.

Forgiveness may be difficult. The offense may be huge or continual or merely unnecessary. However, you're in a prison until you let it go. Recognize the other person doesn't realize you're offended, doesn't care, or has already asked God for forgiveness. They answer to God. And so do you. Take some time to work through the situation and make a conscious choice to forgive. Chad Clifton came back after that injury, played several seasons, and made it into the Packers Hall of Fame.

**EXTRA POINT:**

Dear Lord, help me to choose forgiveness, no matter what the situation.

*Chad Clifton, Left Tackle, Inducted into the Packers Hall of Fame 2016*

# The Block

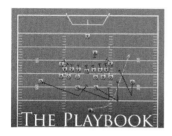

THE PLAYBOOK

**COACH'S CHALLENGE:**

"Some people try to find things in this game that don't exist, but football is only two things—blocking and tackling." Vince Lombardi

A field goal would've tied it, but the Packers decided to go for the victory. Bart Starr made the call. "Thirty-one wedge and I'll carry the ball." With the temperature at 13 below zero, he wouldn't risk anyone slipping on a handoff. To create a hole off Jerry Kramer's left shoulder, Kramer and Bowman needed to move Dallas guard Jethro Pugh out of the way.[61]

Kramer claimed he came off the ball as fast as humanly possible. "I wouldn't swear that I didn't beat the center's snap by a fraction of a second." Pugh's body was a little high, making it easier for Bowman and Kramer to move him. Dallas tackle Willie Townes stayed low but failed to close the middle. Bart charged into the opening and fell into the end zone. "It was the most beautiful sight in the world, seeing Bart lying next to me and seeing the referee in front of me, his arms over his head, signaling the touchdown." Thirteen seconds remained on the clock.

Packer fans ran onto the field, Dallas was furious, and Bart cried. Kramer worried he might not make it safely to the locker room as fans tried to grab his chin strap and gloves for a souvenir. Cameramen crowded into the locker room, but Coach Lombardi kicked them out. The team then knelt and prayed the Lord's Prayer. "And then we exploded, with shouts of joy and excitement," said Kramer, "the marks of battle, the cuts, the bruises, and the blood, all forgotten."[62]

Kramer knew his moment. He was there. He was focused. He was cold, and he was sore, but this was the game. It was a now or never moment for each of them.

Can you live in the moment? What does it take to live in the moment? It takes practice and determination and intuition. Laxness isn't an option because, when the crisis comes, you need wisdom to react quickly. Practiced intuition helps you know what to do. The Bible teaches us to hide God's Word in our hearts so we won't sin against Him (Psalm 119:11). Opportunities to sin come often. Resisting sin requires determination. Instant decisions are often necessary in times of crisis, times when we're exhausted or emotionally taxed. If we haven't trained ourselves, analyzed situations, and experienced making right and wrong decisions, we may slip.

A football player studies the opposition, works with teammates, practices plays, and trains his body. Similarly, we need to learn the ways God works, know the things that easily trip us up, and then fortify ourselves in prayer, worship, and Bible study. When we do, we can make the right block in frigid weather, during exhausting play, with painful bodies, and help the team score the touchdown that wins the championship.

**EXTRA POINT:**

Lord, I'll do what I've never done, but should have, in preparation to make right decisions for my future and my family.

*Jerry Kramer, Guard, Inducted into the Packers Hall of Fame 1975*

# Fumble of Great Worth

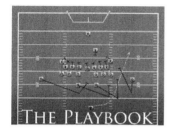

**THE PLAYBOOK**

**FROM THE PLAYBOOK:**

*So I looked for a man among them who would make a wall, and stand in the gap before Me on behalf of the land.*

Ezekiel 22:30

**COACH'S CHALLENGE:**

"The quality of a person's life is in direct proportion to their commitment to excellence, regardless of their chosen field of endeavor." Vince Lombardi

Willie Davis entered the huddle near the end of the game and said, "Alright fellas, somebody's gotta make a play. We gotta get this ball back." The Packers led the Colts 14-10, but Colts quarterback Johnny Unitas was hot. The Colts moved systematically into Packer territory.

Colts linemen had pushed Davis to the outside for most of the game, allowing Unitas to step into the pocket and launch his pass. This time Willie faked to the outside. The guard thought he'd overpowered Willie, but instead, Willie reversed his direction and moved back to the inside to pursue the quarterback. Unitas ran. Davis gave all he could to catch up and punch the ball as he landed on Unitas.

The ball came out, and Dave Robinson picked it up for the Packers.[63]

It was referred to as the Million Dollar Fumble. Willie laughed that a ten-thousand-dollar player had orchestrated it.[64]

A few years earlier, Willie Davis heard on the radio that he'd been traded to Green Bay from the Cleveland Browns. He wasn't happy. Green Bay was considered Siberia. Coaches threatened their players by telling them they'd send them to Green Bay if they didn't perform.

Then Lombardi called him. "Willie, you're going to come to Green Bay, and you're going to play for the Packers."

"Well, Coach, I'd like to think about it."

"No, Willie, you tell me right now. We want you up here. We'd be a good fit for you." Willie found Coach Lombardi the most authoritative and convincing man he'd ever known.[65]

Willie came to Green Bay, and for ten seasons performed as one of the most feared pass rushers in football. He ranked high in sack totals even though records weren't kept during his time. He knew he'd be called on at the end of the game when players were exhausted, so he worked diligently to keep himself in top shape.[66]

Willie stepped up when a play had to be made. In that game with the Colts, he sacked Unitas and punched out the ball. He made the difference in the game. That game sealed the Western Conference Championship for the Packers. Willie revealed the needed play to his teammates and then made it happen.

How often do we see the need and cry out, "Somebody

has to do something. We need to step up!" If no one meets the need, we point the finger of blame at others. But are you in top shape? Are you ready to expend the extra energy and take the risk to obtain a win for your family, your business, your team? Even though you may not earn a lot of money, are you willing to cause the big turnaround even when you feel exhausted and the goal seems unreachable? That's teamwork. That's commitment. That's excellence. Train yourself diligently to be ready and willing to step up.

**EXTRA POINT:**

Dear Lord, guide me so I recognize the needs around me and get prepared to assist.

*Willie Davis, Defensive End, Inducted into the Packers Hall of Fame 1975*

# Call the Butler

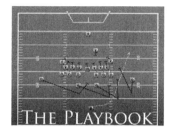

THE PLAYBOOK

**FROM THE PLAYBOOK:**

*O Lord, You have searched me and known me. You know my sitting down and my rising up; You understand my thought afar off.*

Psalm 139:1-2

**COACH'S CHALLENGE:**

"Life's battles don't always go to the stronger or faster man. But sooner or later, the man who wins is the man who thinks he can." Vince Lombardi

On December 26, 1993, the Oakland Raiders lagged 14-0 behind the Packers and lined up on their own 45-yard line in the fourth quarter. Quarterback Vince Evans was chased out of the pocket and threw a screen to Ricky Jordan. He caught the ball at their 38 but fumbled when Packer safety Leroy Butler hit him. Reggie White picked up the fumble but was grabbed and pulled to the sideline by guard Steve Wisniewski. Reggie lateraled to Butler who ran it into the end zone. Packer fans went crazy. The Raiders were stunned. Butler leapt into the stands and into the hearts of Packer fans everywhere.[67]

"It was very spontaneous," said Butler in 2014 at the

unveiling of the new Lambeau Leap Wall just outside Lambeau Field. "I used to dance a lot. This time there was one particular guy whose eyes said 'hug me.'" So he kept going right into the arms of that fan.

At a time when end zone celebrations brought fines, the Lambeau Leap was approved. "You're not showing up the Raiders; you're celebrating with your fans," said Butler at the unveiling. "I thought about the connection with their favorite player. We're signing this over to the fans. I wish Reggie White was here to experience [this]."[68]

Leroy Butler knew the celebration was about the fans, about connection. Packer players have had a love affair with Packer fans for years. The connections of hugging, high-fivin', saying hi, and getting an autograph are important to the fans. The Packers understand their team is owned by their fans, by the community, and they recognize Lambeau Field as a special place. Greta Van Susteren, well-known Fox journalist for many years, said, "Being a Packer fan is like a disease. It's terminal; it never leaves you."[69]

What is your special place? What are your important connections? What stories do you like to tell? Where is your real church—the place where you actually worship? Wonder why so many Packer players and other NFL players share their faith? Because people are listening. This is their connection.

The Lord will come to you in the place where you spend time. He will pursue you until you pursue Him. Think how Butler pursued Jordan, then pursued Reggie to get the lateral. He then pursued the end zone and finally pursued the fans. He made the necessary connections. God is connecting with you right now. Can you see Him? Can you feel Him? Do you hear Him?

**EXTRA POINT:**

Dear Lord, help me to see the connections that give me the opportunity to know You and share who You are.

*Leroy Butler, Safety, Inducted into the Packer Hall of Fame 2007*

# Abundant Life

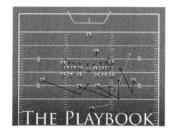

**COACH'S CHALLENGE:**

"The only place success comes before work is in the dictionary." Vince Lombardi

"Dear Lord, don't let me screw up." Those were Larry McCarren's words before he interviewed Packer players on his TV show. The audience prayed the prayer out loud with Larry. Then the signal came, and the show began. My son and I attended several shows, enjoying Larry's insight and humor.

McCarren was the center for the Packers from 1973-84. It is generally reported he earned his nickname, The Rock, by playing 162 consecutive games. He laughs at that and says a college teammate drafted with him called him Rock, the nickname given McCarren in college because of his strenuous workout routine. As rookies, they played a scrimmage with the veteran players, and the coach told them not to take any guff or he'd cut them. McCarren missed a block, so he ran down the veteran player and, in a cheap shot, took him down. The player turned and punched Larry right under the chin. In the replay, all the veterans guffawed at the Rock. The name then stuck.[70]

McCarren and Wayne Larrivee currently announce the radio broadcast of all Packer games, following in the footsteps of Max McGee and Jim Irwin. Of all McCarren does, he enjoys this the most. "Everything revolves around the games, and to be a small part of it is big."

McCarren appreciates what he has and doesn't think more highly of himself than he ought to think. He is recognized as an exceptional analyst, but when he tells the stories of playing for the Packers and broadcasting sports, he always states that at first he "stunk." He was bad. Then he learned and became "acceptable." Finally, he was "okay." He considers himself to have been a good professional football player due to focus, training, and good coaches but says he was never a great player.[71]

What do you think of you? Is it an honest evaluation or influenced by biased thinking? Do you base it on what you do or who you are? The Bible says in Christ we are complete (Colossians 2:10). He has made us acceptable. We aren't worthless; we are worthy because of His love for us. Our performance may still be lousy, but God promises to make our way perfect. It takes cooperation and faith and time to grow, but our value is already established, and we are highly regarded in His eyes.

McCarren worked at his vocation, knowing full well it could improve with practice and training. Our walk with the Lord also requires practice and training. We need to practice listening and obeying daily. The Lord can train us as we read His Word and hear His voice. These methods will help us progress from being "okay" to walking in the superabundant life.

**EXTRA POINT:**

Lord, thank You that as I listen, obey, and steadily and persistently learn to walk in Your ways, my way will be blessed.

*Larry McCarren, Center, Inducted into the Packers Hall of Fame 1992*

# Flourishing Faith

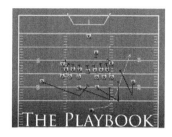

THE PLAYBOOK

**FROM THE PLAYBOOK:**

*The righteous shall flourish like a palm tree, he shall grow like a cedar in Lebanon.*

Psalm 92:12

**COACH'S CHALLENGE:**

"Football is like life—it requires perseverance, self-denial, hard work, sacrifice, dedication, and respect for authority." Vince Lombardi

Packers' defensive end Joe Johnson got in the face of Bears' quarterback Jim Miller during the third quarter of the October 2002 game. His pass went straight up and short; it arrived in the arms of Kabeer Gbaja-Bialmila, the defensive end lovingly known as KGB. The catch occurred on the Packers' 28-yard line, and KGB ran untouched 72 yards to the end zone. The Packers won the game 31-24.[72]

KGB holds the all-time sack record for the Packers. He surpassed Reggie White's record of 68.5 sacks in October 2007, hitting number 69. When he left the team, he'd accumulated 74.5 sacks. His contributions to the team in his rookie season were modest. The following year, after training and giving attention to instruction, he burst out with nine sacks in the first four games. "I had time to grow as a player … I like struggle," he said. "Because I struggled and worked hard, I was ready when my time came."[73]

If you talk to him today, he'd rather not talk about his accomplishments. He prefers to discuss the struggles he went through spiritually and what the Lord has accomplished in his life.

Faith is an interesting commodity. Many consider it a crutch or quirk of culture. They think a person raised in a particular faith irrationally holds on to it like a child with an old, broken toy, smudged but comfortable. However, watching the transformation of someone who discovers the reality of faith is an amazing experience.

KGB began reading the Bible at the challenge of Gill Byrd, a friend from San Diego State. At the end of 2000, KGB gave his life to the Lord. He grew up in Los Angeles with his parents, a twin sister, and three other siblings. Both parents were Muslim until his mom chose Christianity. KGB felt the Muslim faith held more order, and he wanted to be like his dad. Reading the Bible changed that desire. He asked so many questions as he sought the truth, and when Gill Byrd showed him what the Bible said, KGB prayed to the God who created him.[74]

**EXTRA POINT:**

Lord, help me to always seek truth from You, the God who created me.

*Kabeer Gbaja-Biamila, Defensive End, Inducted into the Packers Hall of Fame 2013*

# Stay Calm and Believe

**FROM THE PLAYBOOK:**

*Blessed be the God and Father of our Lord Jesus Christ, the Father of mercies, and God of all comfort; who comforts us in all our tribulation, that we may be able to comfort those who are in any trouble, with the comfort with which we ourselves are comforted by God.*

2 Corinthians 1:3-4

**COACH'S CHALLENGE:**

"Perfection is not attainable, but if we chase perfection we can catch excellence." Vince Lombardi

"It is the most remarkable recovery I have ever seen in my twenty years as a trainer," said Pepper Burress, Packer trainer.[75] The 49ers-Packers Monday night game in October '96 was big. The first play from scrimmage, wide receiver Robert Brooks lined up right side. Edgar Bennett ran a sweep to the left. Brooks took on cornerback Tyrone Drakeford. The cornerback yanked Brooks down, and his right knee buckled. He told the staff to get him off the field quickly so no one would see him cry. He smiled and gave a thumbs-up as the staff carted him to the locker room.

Holmgren confirmed the season-ending injury; Dr. Pat McKenzie said Brooks might never play football again. He'd damaged the patellar tendon, the anterior cruciate ligament, the medial collateral ligament, the meniscus cartilage, and chipped a bone in the knee.[76]

Three weeks earlier, Brooks had a dream. It was twofold. God instructed him to become strong in faith, not middle of the road. God also told Brooks he wouldn't finish the season but assured him the setback wouldn't be permanent. He'd play football again.

Brooks experienced unimaginable pain. "As I was just about ready to pass out, God told me why He had allowed me to be injured." The Lord told him to handle the injury positively, in faith, and to show others that they too could handle troubling times with a positive faith. The Packer chaplain shared 2 Corinthians 1:3-4 with Brooks that night. It confirmed what he'd heard from God.[77]

The next season started on a Monday night. Brooks played that game. He was back.

Brooks missed the Super Bowl for the '96 season, a true disappointment; however, he gained a ministry. Brooks showed others how to walk in faith, trusting in God's ability to heal and to answer prayer. He trusted God and did not fear. He believed and stayed positive, knowing God had already given the answer.

Are you able to believe God when things look hopeless? Robert Brooks heard from God that even though he'd miss the rest of the season, he'd play again. That didn't happen because he was special, but because he stood in a place where many could watch him handle his situation in faith and with a positive attitude. God told him to share it. So if you missed his message in '96 and '97, here it is again. Be comforted with the comfort given to Robert Brooks, and then pass it on.

**EXTRA POINT:**

Thank You, Lord, that I can comfort others in the same way You have comforted and strengthened me.

*Robert Brooks, Wide Receiver, Inducted into the Packer Hall of Fame 2007*

# The Drumbeat

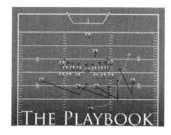

**FROM THE PLAYBOOK:**

*Jesus said, "My sheep hear my voice, and I know them, and they follow Me."*

John 10:27

**COACH'S CHALLENGE:**

"If you're lucky enough to find a guy with a lot of head and a lot of heart, he's never going to come off the field second." Vince Lombardi

Best friends. Frank Winters and Brett Favre. In 1992, Frankie from New Jersey and Brett from Louisiana spent more time together than anyone else on the Packers' team. Frankie, Brett, and Mark Chmura became known as the Three Amigos for several seasons, spending their off days and vacations together. Eventually, the Packers let Chmura go due to a much-publicized indiscretion. Frankie and Brett remained best friends. As Brett's center, Frankie probably knew Brett's cadence and calls better than he did. When Brett did a hard count and the opposing team jumped offside, Frankie knew to snap the ball to get in a play before the whistle ended the opportunity.[78]

The best friends were also masters of practical jokes and

nicknames. They continually pulled jokes on each other and other team members. Frank became known as Ol' Bag of Donuts due to comments made by famous Monday Night Football announcer John Madden.[79] The nickname stuck. Brett was the Gunslinger.

Can you read the person you spend the most time with as well as Frankie could read Brett? Can you flow with your spouse, boss, parent, child, or sibling day in and out? Sometimes we rub each other the wrong way. Flowing like a well-oiled machine with another person takes time and effort.

Can you do that with the Lord? Is that possible? Can you spend so much time with Him that you sense His moves before He speaks or nudges you in a direction? That's the way a sports team becomes a champion. You can become a true extension of God's purpose, love, and hand in the world if you learn His ways. In Psalm 103:7, God speaks of those who knew His acts and those who knew His ways. We all love the acts, and well we should. But if we know His ways, we can help extend His acts.

It doesn't happen overnight, but over time you can and should expect to know the Lord's cadence, to recognize His still small voice, and to act quickly to obey His promptings.

**EXTRA POINT:**

Lord, I'll invest the time necessary to hear Your voice, I'll yield to Your Spirit, and I'll walk in Your ways.

*Frank Winters, Center, Inducted into the Packers Hall of Fame 2008*

# Responsibility

**FROM THE PLAYBOOK:**

*Jesus said, "Most assuredly, I say to you, unless a grain of wheat falls into the ground and dies, it remains alone; but if it dies, it produces much grain."*

John 12:24

**COACH'S CHALLENGE:**

"Mental toughness is many things and rather difficult to explain. Its qualities are sacrifice and self-denial. Also, most importantly, it is combined with a perfectly disciplined will that refuses to give in. It's a state of mind—you could call it 'character in action.'" Vince Lombardi

"I was 20 when I met him [Lombardi] and remember when he told me, 'You are responsible for yourself.'" Linebacker Fred Carr took that responsibility. He played in 140 consecutive games. "Playing in every game meant that you stood up and answered the bell every Sunday." That he did, recovering 25 fumbles and blocking three field goals and two extra points.[80]

A friend gave me a painting of three Packer players. I didn't recognize any of them, so I did some research. First, I found pictures of players who had worn the jersey numbers in the photo. I then searched for the year when all three numbers were worn. Eventually, I identified the three players. One was Fred Carr, number 53. So I see him every day now.

Fred Carr took responsibility for himself. That's impressive in this day and age. So many want prosperity and provision handed to them. Carr worked, trained, and disciplined himself in order to walk worthy of the accolades he received. So many have capability similar to the amazing potential an undeveloped seed holds. However, if the seed remains in your hand or on the shelf, it will never produce that for which it was designed. It actually has to go in the ground, shed its outer shell, and draw nutrients from the soil so its marvelous capability can spring forth.

What is the soil in which you need to plant yourself? You know great successes lie within you, callings and purposes you long to fulfill. Where are you planted? Have you placed yourself where you can discipline, focus, and develop what God has purposed for you? That may be a field of study, an area of practice, or a focus each day. If you have no idea where to start, begin by immersing yourself in the Word of God, the Bible. As you absorb His words, they'll spring up in wisdom, guidance, direction, and connections you never dreamed of. The difference between success and status quo is taking responsibility to be what and where God wants you to be.

**EXTRA POINT:**

Dear Lord, I commit to a life of discipline and responsibility so I can walk in the wonderful blessings You have planned for me.

*Fred Carr, Linebacker, Inducted into Packers Hall of Fame 1983*

# Twists and Turns
# of Life

**FROM THE PLAYBOOK:**

*And a vision appeared to Paul in the night. A man of Macedonia stood and pleaded with him, saying, "Come over to Macedonia and help us."*

Acts 16:9

**COACH'S CHALLENGE:**

"The measure of who we are is what we do with what we have." Vince Lombardi

Both teams piled up a yard short of the end zone. Ahman Green, who carried the ball, first tried to go through the pile, then up and over it. Neither worked. Finally, he pulled back and muscled his way around the side of the scrum and into the end zone to score against the 49ers—a typical day for Ahman Green.[81]

Another day, against the Broncos, Brett Favre backed from the line of scrimmage, the Packers' two-yard line. In a misdirection play, he tossed the ball to Green in the end zone. Green saw a hole in the defense and later said, "I just turned on the jet." Untouched, he reached the other end zone for six points. Usually, he dodged and twisted with great balance and tenacity to elude the opposing players. That's how he broke Jim Taylor's record of most rushing yards for a Green Bay running back. Taylor said he and Green were old-school running backs. "You have to be willing to hit people and take the punishment and dish it out."[82]

I first met Ahman Green when he attended a Jump Rope for Heart event at the school where I taught. A few of my students and I visited with him for about 20 minutes. He indicated he wanted to be a teacher when he left football.

For a time, he worked as a teacher intern at DePere High School. "The big thing I took from my coaches and teachers was to be prepared and do your best in whatever you're doing. That's what I've tried to do."[83] Green worked on a master's degree in leadership administration with the goal of becoming a school principal or athletic director.

Ahman is still connected with football and the Packers. Currently, he is co-host for the local Packer sports show, Locker Room, with Burke Griffin.[84] Green's dream of being a teacher may still reside in him. It will be interesting to see what he continues to do.

We have so many possibilities and dreams in our hearts and minds, but life's events take us in directions we may have never considered. We often determine to go one way and yet find ourselves going another direction. It may be for the positive to the delight of our soul. It could also be for the negative to the regret of our heart. Much we never dreamed of occurs in our lives.

So what are we to do?

Submit all your dreams and plans to the Lord. Ask Him to help you plant the seed of that which has never occurred but still pulls at your heart. He can still cause it to take root or come to fruition. On the other hand, if you find yourself so amazed by your current path and delighted to be where you are, give thanks to God and ask Him to help you assist others as they pursue their dreams and fulfill their purpose.

May we never be the one who says to ourselves or to others, "Well, that's life." Instead, let's believe and trust God for the full growth of what He wants to provide.

**EXTRA POINT:**

Father, here I am on this road in life. I give this walk to You and ask You to work in me to fulfill every plan You have for me and every dream I thought was lost.

*Ahman Green, Running Back, Inducted into the Packers Hall of Fame 2014*

# Questions

**COACH'S CHALLENGE:**

"When we place our dependence in God, we are unencumbered, and we have no worry. In fact, we may even be reckless, insofar as our part in the production is concerned. This confidence, this sureness of action, is both contagious and an aid to the perfect action. The rest is in the hands of God—and this is the same God, gentlemen, who has won all His battles up to now." Vince Lombardi

Johnny Holland relished the game of football and played it well. Drafted by the Packers in the second round, Holland made the All-Rookie team his first season. Years later, when an injury sidelined his playing days, he turned to coaching and enjoyed a successful career working with several NFL teams. But it was another turn that made all the difference. He hungered for accolades, awards, recognition, big contracts, and he was capable of bringing them all in. But something was missing. Football didn't meet his deepest need. Somehow he knew there was more to life. But what?

Then Holland heard Reggie White speak at Texas A&M University, the school where Holland attained an All-American selection both his junior and senior years.

Reggie challenged those listening, "If you were to die today, where would you spend eternity?" Johnny considered that question and heeded Reggie's advice. He committed his life to Jesus Christ and found a peace he'd never experienced. He also received strength to face whatever adversity came his way. "Finally, God gave me a new perspective of the game I love. No matter what uniform I wear, I'm dedicated to giving 100 percent all the time because God expects nothing less than my best effort."[85]

Amazing, isn't it? We meet all our dreams, reach all our goals, and then discover that bit of unfulfillment, the confusion of why it doesn't satisfy even though it's what we've always wanted. Some people continue trying to meet goals. Some fill their lives with fun. Some reach out to unsavory answers that can have disappointing ends—drinking, drugs, or destructive relationships. Some do good: they volunteer, focus on their family, and help those in need. However, in Christ, we don't do good to please God and others. We want to do good and are led to do good because He is good and because He's in us and with us.

The true answer to one's purpose is to envelop that purpose in God. Let Him take it and guide it, make it possible or change it. It's quite exciting. It's truly an adventure because then those desires you had as a young person are shaped, directed, and come to fruition in amazing ways with amazing results.

Consider Reggie's question, and listen to God's voice within. The God of the Bible has good things planned for you that will fill you with immense satisfaction and joy.

**EXTRA POINT:**

Lord Jesus, I ask You to come into my heart and make the changes I need so I can walk in the paths of peace and purpose You designed for me before I was born.

*Johnny Holland, Linebacker, Inducted into the Packers Hall of Fame 2001*

# Gaining a Following

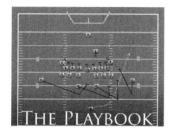

THE PLAYBOOK

**FROM THE PLAYBOOK:**

*Therefore let us pursue the things which make for peace and the things by which one may edify another.*

Romans 14:19

**COACH'S CHALLENGE:**

"Having the capacity to lead is not enough. The leader must be willing to use it." Vince Lombardi

William Henderson, known as Hendo, lined up on Favre's right, Ahman Green on his left. Almost halfway through the fourth quarter against the Baltimore Ravens in the 2001 season, the Packers faced second and eight. Favre rolled to his left, faking to Green. Henderson made a beeline to the left, bumping one defender headed toward Favre, then continued straight for Ray Lewis and stopped his forward movement. Favre tossed a pass to Freeman, and the Packers gained a first down on the Ravens' 48-yard line.[86]

Henderson, an outstanding fullback and lead blocker, was an unsung hero for the Packers' offense. I always knew that when the running back followed him, he'd make a first down, get free for a great run, or at least gain a few yards beyond the line of scrimmage. William Henderson could read the defense and lead the way. Running backs Edgar Bennett, Dorsey Levens, and Ahman Green all achieved 1,000-yard seasons with Henderson as their lead blocker. Henderson also caught many passes out of the backfield and kept defenders away from Brett Favre.[87]

Being on offense is more than charging forward. The key to gaining ground is reading the defense, knowing the opposition's moves. Henderson could probably feel the running back right behind him.

Having a guide—someone to prepare the way for us, to run interference, and to see the path ahead—is an incredible blessing. Our God is the one who sees ahead and provides the direction. The question is, are we right behind the Lord following His lead? Hesitation in football generally doesn't end well. The bottom line is trust. When you walk continually in trust, the journey is fairly easy, but when you've often been tackled in life, trust becomes more difficult.

Life requires so many choices and decisions that we naturally try to protect ourselves. It doesn't always work, does it? Sadly, the life of hesitating, with the intention to protect ourselves, results in more tackles. Moving forward trusting our fullback, the Lord, will result in more first downs and touchdowns.

**EXTRA POINT:**

Lord, You are the one I will follow on a daily basis. You see the openings, and I will stay close. I trust You.

*William Henderson, Fullback, Inducted into the Packers Hall of Fame 2011*

# Motor City Marvel

**FROM THE PLAYBOOK:**

*You will not need to fight in this battle. Position yourselves, stand still and see the salvation of the Lord who is with you, O Judah and Jerusalem! Do not fear or be dismayed; tomorrow go out against them, for the Lord is with you.*

2 Chronicles 20:17

**COACH'S CHALLENGE:**

"We didn't lose the game; we just ran out of time." Vince Lombardi

I sat on the couch with my ear to the radio as it broadcast the Packers' game in real time while the HD TV was delayed several seconds. I often do this when I feel the need to pray for the Packers.

It was late, and my husband was asleep. My son didn't want to see the Packers lose and went to his room. I tried to face succumbing to the Detroit Lions for the second time this season. All my siblings are Lions' fans, and I'd have to acknowledge their rejoicing. I prayed even though precious few seconds remained on the clock. We did have the ball, so there was still a chance. Extremely thin, but a chance. The center snapped the ball, Aaron Rodgers backpedaled, and then he went down. The end of the game. This loss hurt.

But wait, the ref had thrown a flag. The game couldn't end on a defensive penalty, so I tuned back into the radio. Indeed, the ref called a face-mask penalty on the defense. I watched the replay on the TV and could see that some might argue with the call, but the player's hand had touched Aaron's face. The clock had run out, but the Packers were given one more play, an untimed down. Aaron dodged back and forth, and then, on the Packers' 40-yard line, Aaron let it fly—a Hail Mary pass. On the radio, Wayne Larrivee spoke ahead of what I saw on TV. "Richard Rodgers got it! It is a touchdown! Unbelievable!"

I screamed, "He got it. He got it. We won! We won! We won!" Then I watched the delayed view of Richard Rodgers backing into the fray. The Lions didn't get in front of him, and the ball fell right to him. Most importantly, he retained possession. We won! Who could believe it! Who could sleep in this house? I wondered if the skies wavered above Wisconsin with the screams that rose across the state. What a comeback! The Packers hadn't led once in regulation, and yet we won the game.

The ball not only traveled 60 yards down the field, but it also arched probably 60 feet in the air. Later, Richard Rodgers said he and Aaron had practiced that move three times before the game, and twice he'd caught the ball. He wasn't in the group that leapt for the ball so rarely caught, but the Lions failed to surround the Packers. They remained in the background while Rodgers just backed in and caught the winning touchdown.[88]

What an unlikely win. Packer fans know Aaron Rodgers, a future Hall of Famer, is so capable of winning when all looks lost. Still, it rarely happens like this game. We dream of such moments: all is lost, down to the wire, the world watching, and we pull off the win with the dynamic, incredible, who-would-have-ever-thought-possible move. The classic comeback. The stuff of diehard persistence, of unmatched determination, the wonder of marvelous stories. It happened in Detroit—for Green Bay.

It also happened 2,000 years ago on a much greater stage when Jesus died on the cross. All was lost. He was the hope of the world, and now He was gone. Sin would reign in the world. The Enemy had killed the Messiah. The disciples hid. They grieved.

And then the impossible happened.

How could it be? Jesus was alive! He was back. Victory unimaginable. Joy indescribable. But it happened! His victory wasn't a one-season, one-game miracle. It was the miracle of all time, not making only one team happy but paving the way for everyone to live free from bondage and pain forever and to know purpose, fulfillment, and joy. A football game is temporary, even though it can create a forever memory. But the return to life, Jesus' victory over death, is a forever fact and a daily provision for every person for all time.

**EXTRA POINT:**

Lord, I rejoice in the miracle of resurrection that You gave me so I might have life and have it abundantly.

*Aaron Rodgers, Quarterback, Future Inductee into the Packers Hall of Fame*

# The Snow Bowl

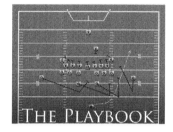

THE PLAYBOOK

**FROM THE PLAYBOOK:**

*Whenever I am afraid, I will trust in You.*

Psalm 56:3

**COACH'S CHALLENGE:**

"The good Lord gave you a body that can stand most anything. It's your mind you have to convince." Vince Lombardi

The Packers faced third and 22 in the swirling snow. They already had turnovers and missed field goals. This time, quarterback Lynn Dickey pulled back and connected with tight end Paul Coffman for 19 yards. Dickey then kept the ball and ran for the first score of the game. The few fans present knew the Tampa Bay Bucs were the opposing team, but no one could see them in their white uniforms and white helmets.

The reason? A foot of snow had fallen before the game and several inches during that game on December 1, 1985, while the winds gusted to 40 mph. The maintenance crew shoveled the yard lines between plays. The Packers were the only ones visible in their green and gold. For probably the first time in its history, the stadium had less than 20,000 in attendance.[89]

In the third quarter, Dickey and Coffman connected again for 19 yards. After two more plays, fullback Gerry Ellis ran 35 yards for another touchdown. At game's end, Dickey had thrown for 299 yards, and the team had gained 31 first downs. The Bucs had five first downs and gained only 65 yards.[90]

*The New York Times* headline said it all: Packers 21, Bucs 0, Snow 16.[91] Our family had moved to Wisconsin less than a year before the Snow Bowl, and we'd quickly become Packer fans. On that day, we were driving home from a Thanksgiving visit with family in the Detroit area. We were out of range to hear the game on the radio. Our drive was clear and dry until we reached northeastern Wisconsin, where we encountered a foot of snow and picked up the game news.

Some storms arise suddenly. Anyone who has driven in blinding snow knows how treacherous and scary it can be. The football players probably didn't fear for their safety in the game, but direction proved problematic. They looked for the ball to arrive out of the white, and then they continued in the path the ball traveled—a unique experience for each team. The blowing snow and cold created havoc for the Bucs, but the Packers enjoyed the game.

Sometimes surprising events hit us like whiteout storms. They blind and often scare us. Terrible accidents may occur if we can't see the way. The terror we feel is paralyzing. Yet we have someone within to guide us.

As fear rises, we can cry out to the Lord, "Whenever I'm

afraid, I will trust in You." It's important to train ourselves to hear His voice within us. It's wise to practice trust over and over. A football player practices a variety of scenarios daily until they become second nature. Well-practiced movements and reactions occur almost instinctively.

The Holy Spirit works within us as we daily ponder each decision. As we lean in to perceive His direction, we develop what is known as a gut feeling. When a life-threatening situation occurs, we'll have a well-practiced ability to sense His leading, survive the whiteout storm, and emerge with a victory.

**EXTRA POINT:**

Lord, You have created me to hear Your voice within. I desire to learn how You speak and to follow Your nudges and direction.

*Lynn Dickey, Quarterback, Inducted into the Packers Hall of Fame 1992*

*Paul Coffman, Tight End, Inducted into the Packers Hall of Fame 1994*

*Gerry Ellis, Fullback, Inducted into the Packers Hall of Fame 1994*

# Time to Turn Loose

**FROM THE PLAYBOOK:**

*Now no chastening seems to be joyful for the present, but painful; nevertheless, afterward it yields the peaceable fruit of righteousness to those who have been trained by it.*

Hebrews 12:11

**COACH'S CHALLENGE:**

"Success is never final. Failure is never fatal. It is courage that counts." Vince Lombardi

The Packers' 14-10 halftime lead in Super Bowl I rattled Lombardi. The possibility of failure loomed. Willie Davis recounts that his coach looked terrified in the locker room— his face sweaty, his cheeks pale, and his eyes tired. Shaking, but determined, Lombardi applauded the team for playing cautiously in the first half and adapting to the Kansas City Chiefs to avoid mistakes. "Now I want them to adjust to you. Let the Chiefs have the burden of trying to stop you. I want you to go out there and play 30 minutes of Green Bay Packer football!"[92]

Lombardi's challenge set the team free, and they owned

the rest of the game. Their confidence spoke in their play. Max McGee and Bart Starr were energized to improvise. The defense got in Chiefs' quarterback Len Dawson's face—pressuring, sacking, hitting, and hurrying him. Safety Willie Wood intercepted a Dawson pass early in the second half, returning it to the five-yard line. Elijah Pitts scored on a five-yard run, making the score 21-10. McGee scored on a pass from Starr, then Pitts sprinted into the end zone again to cap the score at 35-10. The Packers reigned as World Champions.[93]

Someone once asked Elijah Pitts if Lombardi scared him the first time he heard him. "He scared me the last time I heard him too," Pitts quipped. The son of a sharecropper in Arkansas, Pitts attended a small college before Green Bay selected him in the thirteenth round of the 1961 draft.[94] Pitts and Dave Robinson shared a small house in Green Bay and became best friends. Robinson said of Pitts, "He was Vince's kind of player: athletic, smart, and durable." Lombardi used him on special teams, as a leading tackler, and as running back.[95]

As for the famous Packer power sweep, developed by Lombardi, it took Pitts two years to settle down and run it correctly. He often swept right by Kramer and Thurston. Like Thurston, Pitts displayed enough confidence to get up and sing at the training camp dinners.[96]

Pitts was well rounded and proved himself to Lombardi. Lombardi put confidence in his team, and in Super Bowl I, he turned them loose after trying to hold them in. Confidence and freedom. What a delicate balance. Does confidence bring freedom, or does freedom bring confidence? Or do they go hand in hand?

Confidence is built by discipline, by paying attention and developing correct methods over time. Pitts developed confidence, as did all Lombardi's players. They worked together, squirmed under their coach's thumb together, learned their individual roles, and became a collective personality. When that discipline moved to confidence, Lombardi gave them freedom. Even in the Super Bowl, Lombardi held them close for the first half. Then he let them loose to do as they were trained. He had faith in their training and in their confidence. He could trust their freedom.

Our walk with the Lord is similar. Some disciplines seem so confining. We feel we are denying ourselves when we thought we should be free. We occasionally fear freedom as much as we desire it. But when we learn our role, walk in our calling, cooperate with, pray for, and love our teammates, the Lord will give us freedom. When He does, we'll go out and excel in the things He's trained us for and become champions for the Lord.

**EXTRA POINT:**

Father, I submit myself to Your training so that when the time for freedom arrives, I'll be totally pleasing to You.

*Elijah Pitts, Running Back, Inducted into the Packers Hall of Fame 1979*

# Blazing Trails On and Off the Field

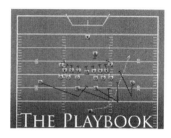

THE PLAYBOOK

**COACH'S CHALLENGE:**

"Gentlemen, I just want you to know that win, lose, or draw, you're my football team." Vince Lombardi

It was Herb Adderley's rookie year as a running back from Michigan State. During the Thanksgiving game with Detroit, the starting left cornerback suffered injury. Lombardi announced at halftime he needed to replace the left corner with his best athlete. He walked over and told Adderley to do the best he could. Shocked and unprepared to play defense, Adderley returned to the game. With no idea what to do, he survived the third quarter. In the fourth quarter, he intercepted Lions' quarterback Jim Ninowski, setting up the game-winning touchdown by Paul Hornung. Adderley blazed a trail, becoming one of the best cornerbacks in NFL history.[97]

Adderley said he thought about Coach Lombardi every day. The principles and attitudes he espoused were lodged in Adderley's thinking even more deeply than what his father taught him. What especially endeared Lombardi to Adderley was his quiet insistence that Green Bay integrate the black players. Adderley, Willie Davis, and Elijah Pitts weren't allowed to live in the city limits of Green Bay in 1961. At that time, civil rights problems raged throughout the country. The three Packer players lived in a one-bedroom apartment next to an exterminating company, the fumes from its chemicals ever present. One player slept in the bedroom, one on the couch, and the third on a cot.

Lombardi went to the team president and quietly demanded fair housing for his players. "Lombardi had zero tolerance for racism." Lombardi became the trailblazer who slowly integrated Green Bay.[98]

Trailblazers are often bombastic, but some also work quietly behind the scenes. They simply have the strong inner passion that right is right and wrong is wrong. Few gray areas exist with them. They're often misunderstood, often resisted, but they're persistent. They make changes for the good. The work doesn't always go quickly, but trailblazers work steadily. They do not give up easily.

Many people support trailblazers; many criticize them. But progress usually doesn't happen without trailblazers. History reveals this is in every area of life. We need them, and we need to appreciate them. The Bible says, "The kingdom of God suffers violence, and the violent take it by force" (Matthew 11:12). This verse doesn't open the door for violence; instead, it shows that accomplishing God's work requires continual, consistent forcefulness in the ways of the Spirit. This might be in prayer, in reaching people with the truth of the Bible, or in making it possible for others to live free in their culture.

I think God likes trailblazers.

**EXTRA POINT:**

Thank You, Lord, for those who blaze the trails we need to travel. Help us to recognize them and to pray for them. Give us the wisdom to be trailblazers if indeed You have called us to that task.

*Herb Adderley, Defensive Back, Inducted into the Packers Hall of Fame 1981*

# Drive to Thrive

**FROM THE PLAYBOOK:**

*Your word is a lamp to my feet and a light to my path.*

Psalm 119:105

**COACH'S CHALLENGE:**

"Individual commitment to a group effort—that is what makes a team work, a company work, a society work, a civilization work." Vince Lombardi

It looked unlikely if not impossible. On the Packers' 24-yard line in September of the 2009 season, Aaron Rodgers took the ball, dropped back, and fired a pass from the 15-yard line. St. Louis rookie Bradley Fletcher ran next to Donald Driver, grabbing his right arm and interfering with Driver's ability to catch the pass. Driver reached up and grabbed the ball with his left hand, pulled it in next to his head, and fell to the ground just short of the Rams' 30-yard line without letting go—one of his greatest catches among hundreds of his career receptions.[99]

I never tired of hearing Wayne Larrivee and Larry McCarren, radio broadcasters of Packer games, almost swallow their mics and yell over and over, "It's Donald

Driver! In the end zone! What a play! What a catch!"

Packer fans everywhere consider Driver their friend, and the excitement and the memories he brought to the game never wane. Whether it's his speed or tenacity, a short or long route, Favre or Rodgers throwing the ball, a one-handed or two-handed catch, middle of the field or along the sideline with his toes barely in bounds, catching in the end zone or having a long run after the catch, surrounded by several defenders or all alone with no one to stop him, a little dance or a Lambeau Leap—every memory warms and thrills the heart.

Donald Driver was drafted in the seventh round. When the Packers handed him a contract that would take care of his family for the rest of his life, he decided he'd never wear another uniform. He surpassed Sterling Sharpe's record of 595 receptions and became the all-time leader in receiving yards and receptions.[100]

Donald Driver is a gem. His tenacity on the field was matched only by his tenacity in life. Driver spent much of his childhood homeless, living in U-Haul trucks, hotels, friends' houses, and on the street. Whatever his family had or didn't have, his mom always told him that God would get them out of the situation. Hardships made him highly appreciative of everything he gained and taught him to trust God. He believes God told him to retire as a Green Bay Packer.[101]

Tough times always seem to go one of two ways. We can be resentful and hardened, or we can be grateful and determined. Of course, gradations and varieties of reactions exist within those responses. Becoming discouraged and jealous of others is easy when hard times come. The challenge is to stay gracious and hopeful.

Not everyone achieves the level of success that Driver attained. He experienced both depths and heights, but he never forgot to be grateful. He had to believe during the hard times that life would get better. What is it about belief that seems to pave the way to success? It's like casting a rope up ahead, into the future, and then following that rope forward, upward. The Bible says God's Word is a light to our path. Paths get murky all the time, but belief in the Lord and trust in the Bible shed enough light on our path to advance one step at a time.

What we innately long for does exist. God places that knowledge and craving within His creation. As babies, we long for nurture and food—the desire placed within us to survive. As we grow, we long for fulfillment, love, and purpose. God placed those desires, dreams, and purposes within us, and we find fulfillment as we reach for Him, just as our needs were met when we reached for our parents as babies.

Donald Driver possessed the drive to seek purpose and provision and trusted God to get him there. He thrived as a result. His example can encourage each of us.

**EXTRA POINT:**

Dear Lord, I reach for You, trusting that You'll guide me into the places and purposes where I can bless those around me.

*Donald Driver, Wide Receiver, Inducted into the Packers Hall of Fame 2017*

# Make Known Your Request

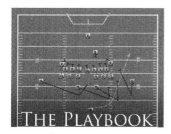

**FROM THE PLAYBOOK:**

*Jesus said, "Until now you have asked nothing in My name. Ask, and you will receive, that your joy may be full."*

John 16:24

**COACH'S CHALLENGE:**

"If you'll not settle for anything less than your best, you will be amazed at what you can accomplish in your lives." Vince Lombardi

Three Packer players charged Len Dawson, Kansas City quarterback, in the third quarter of Super Bowl I. Willie Wood dropped back. Dawson managed to throw the pass to his tight end, Fred Arbanas. Arbanas confidently turned to grab the ball, but instead of being right there, the ball was behind him. "The only thing I saw after that was the bottom of Willie's cleats running away from me. It's kind of a recurring nightmare."[102]

The blitz package was the only addition Lombardi made at half time. Although the Packers held the lead 14-

10, the Chiefs had dominated the first half. The Packers were successful stopping them on the ground but not in the passing game. The Packers had played tight, uptight. Lombardi made it clear that defeat was unacceptable. Wood had even dropped an easy interception in the first half.

The interception in the third quarter came on Kansas City's third down. Willie Wood took it on the Packer 45-yard line and zigzagged 50 yards, landing a few yards short of the goal line. Lombardi said the play changed the personality of the game. Dawson said it was the number one play of his whole career that he wished he could have back. The Packers went on to win 35-10.[103]

Willie Wood played twelve seasons with the Packers and never missed a game. He made Pro Bowl eight times and had 48 interceptions. He was the last man to make the 1960 roster. Back then, only 34 men made the team, unlike the 53-man rosters today. Plus, Wood wasn't drafted. He wrote a letter to four teams, and only Green Bay responded. Although Wood played quarterback at USC, Lombardi made him a free safety.[104]

His stellar career resulted from writing a letter and taking a chance to ask for a chance despite the odds against him. But Wood asked, and Vince Lombardi answered. Two major elements of prayer are asking and believing. Some beg but don't believe. Some believe God sees our need but don't ask Him for help.

Jesus told us to ask so our joy would be full. How wonderful is that? First John 5:14-15 tells us we can be confident that if we ask according to His will, He hears us, and if He hears us, then we'll receive what we asked for. Often we stumble in prayer, too quickly assuming that what we asked wasn't His will. The Bible consists of the Old and New Testaments. The word *testament* means "will." The Bible is God's will. And you can safely and confidently make your request if it lines up with His Word. Step out, no matter the odds, and ask so your joy may be full.

**EXTRA POINT:**

Thank You, Lord, that I can freely and confidently make my requests known to You.

*Willie Wood, Safety, Inducted into the Packers Hall of Fame 1977*

# Return to Life

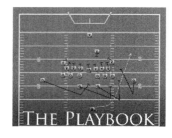

THE PLAYBOOK

**FROM THE PLAYBOOK:**

*Likewise the Spirit also helps in our weaknesses. For we do not know what we should pray for as we ought, but the Spirit Himself makes intercession for us with groanings which cannot be uttered.*

Romans 8:26

**COACH'S CHALLENGE:**

"I believe in God." Vince Lombardi

Lionel Aldridge's Super Bowl ring disappeared one night while he slept out in the middle of nowhere. At that moment, realizing his great loss, he cried out, "Help me! I'll accept help from anyone."

An anchor on the Packers' defensive line in the sixties, the standout end towered at 6'3" and weighed 255 pounds. In the 1965 game for the title against the Browns, Aldridge and the defensive line held running back Jim Brown to only 50 yards. Aldridge's nine seasons with the Packers were outstanding. He finished his playing career with two seasons in San Diego and became a broadcaster.

Throughout his playing and broadcasting careers, though, his friends noticed some severe mood changes. Eventually, Aldridge became homeless, harassed by frightening and confusing voices in his head. The turning point came when his Super Bowl ring, a connection to the success he once had, disappeared.

Aldridge turned to the Bible and found courage to connect with old friends who helped commit him to a hospital. The diagnosis was paranoid schizophrenia. "I did recover. Not without setbacks and relapses, not without moments when I thought I could never again face life, but I did get well with the help of friends, doctors who found the right medication to help me, and the voice of a loving God."

He began traveling the country, speaking about mental illness, recovery, and the Lord. Then in 1985, on the anniversary of the Packers' first Super Bowl victory, his old teammates presented him with a replica of the ring he'd lost. "I knew that day that I had returned."[105]

His malady wasn't attributed to football injury and impact, but many Packer players and other NFL players have suffered debilitation from concussions and other injuries. Football is a tough sport, and thankfully, the NFL has established concussion protocol and set aside funds to assist players.

Mental illness is a terrible condition for anyone to deal with. As Aldridge discovered, he needed to cry out for help at some point. Strangely, he recognized his need only after he lost his Super Bowl ring—that one connection with his best self. Then he had to submit to wise counsel and assistance. He knew the most important aspect was the undergirding of the Lord's love.

This strengthening love is available no matter the desperation of our condition. The journey back to who we really know we are may be longer than we anticipate, but the Lord walks with us and gives us the persistence necessary to overcome the many obstacles we'll encounter. If you or somebody you love suffers from mental illness, do what the Holy Spirit does. Help them. The word *help* in the Greek means to "pull together with against." The Holy Spirit steps in, grabs hold of healing with you, and pulls together with you against that which would defeat you.

Lionel Aldridge went from heaven to hell and back again. "If you're going through hell, don't stop" is a popular saying. Lionel is a powerful voice of one who stopped for a while, then kept going and came out of it. Let him be your inspiration.

**EXTRA POINT:**

Lord, I will trust You to bring me out of the pit I'm in, no matter whose fault it is that I'm here. And, Lord, help me to recognize another's dilemma and be a friend who will come alongside and help that person make it back to fullness of life.

*Lionel Aldridge, Defensive End, Inducted into the Packers Hall of Fame 1998*

# Friends in High Places

**COACH'S CHALLENGE:**

"You are the greatest team in the NFL today. I mean it."
Vince Lombardi

The military draft trumped the NFL draft, and Paul Hornung was called up along with Ray Nitschke and Boyd Dowler by the Army Reserve to active service. Fortunately, President John F. Kennedy was a Packer fan. Vince Lombardi actually put in a call to JFK requesting leave for the players to participate in the 1961 championship game with the New York Giants. Kennedy's reply? "Paul Hornung isn't going to win the war on Sunday, but the football fans of this country deserve the two best teams on the field that day." All three players were given leave.

Hornung, the MVP that day, scored 19 points,

demonstrating his amazing versatility as a football player. He scored one touchdown and kicked three field goals and four extra points. Lombardi characterized him as "the most versatile man who ever played the game."[106]

Lombardi said Hornung could smell the goal line. The coach perfected the power sweep, a yard gainer, with Hornung as Mr. Outside and Jim Taylor as Mr. Inside. Lombardi said, "It's my number-one play because it requires all eleven men to play as one to make it succeed, and that's what 'team' means." The pulling guards block; the lead guard makes a hole. Depending on the direction of the defense, the players travel to the right or left, inside or outside.

Lombardi made the players practice the power sweep at least twice every day so it would become second nature to them. Hornung said, "It gave everybody enough responsibility that you took it upon yourself to do the best you could. And it became the best play in football."[107]

In the 1965 title game against the Browns, the Packers shifted their blocking on the power sweep in the third quarter, confusing the Browns' defense. Kramer and Thurston plowed through linebackers, enabling Hornung to run through mud and snow for a touchdown, sealing a 23-12 win.[108]

Known as the Golden Boy for his good looks and marvelous ability, Hornung was suspended the entire 1963 season for gambling on the game. He also got in trouble for antics outside the game. He appreciated that Lombardi was tough on discipline but still full of love. The players knew Lombardi loved them like a dad and disciplined them like one.[109]

We don't often put discipline hand in hand with love,

and yet discipline brings out the best in us. Water released full blast out of a spigot is less effective than water channeled through a hose and given direction. Lombardi and all other successful coaches understand that great energy and ability are wasted without discipline. The Bible speaks to this in Hebrews, relating our training in the Lord to the discipline administered by our fathers. That discipline prepares us for life. It's rarely exciting or fun, but it trains us to be mature and able to handle responsibility.

**EXTRA POINT:**

Dear Lord, I yield to Your discipline for the training of my heart and mind that I may serve You well.

*Paul Hornung, Halfback, Inducted into the Packers Hall of Fame 1975*

# Exercising Authority

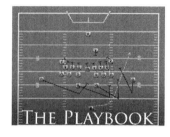

THE PLAYBOOK

**FROM THE PLAYBOOK:**

Jesus said, *"For assuredly, I say to you, whoever says to this mountain, 'Be removed and be cast into the sea,' and does not doubt in his heart, but believes that those things he says will be done, he will have whatever he says."*

Mark 11:23

**COACH'S CHALLENGE:**

"Confidence is contagious. So is lack of confidence." Vince Lombardi

Johnnie Gray tackled. He accumulated over 100 tackles in three of his nine seasons as a safety with the Packers. Recovering 20 fumbles, he was tied for second place with Ray Nitschke while Willie Davis held first place with 21. Gray also had 22 interceptions.[110] He played with authority.

Currently, he spends time each game on the Packers' sideline as uniform inspector. Every NFL team has "fashion police" who make sure players are dressed professionally and wear NFL-licensed gear.

When there's a violation, Gray doesn't tackle or intercept. He writes it up, filling out the forms after warm-ups, during the first quarter, and after the game. According to Akil Coad, NFL's manager of football operations, "The inspector helps the player not get fined. He's there for the players. Listen to him, they won't get fined." Those fines start at $5,000.00.[111]

Authority flowed from Johnnie Gray in whatever position he held. In the past, he's worked as an instructional aide for cognitively disabled children. In addition to inspection duties, he provides game analysis on radio and TV and serves on the board of directors of the Packers.

Authority can be expressed physically, in writing, and in words. Authority may grow over time as confidence increases. It also may come with the position a person holds. In the Bible, authority is most often expressed in words. We're given authority because we belong to the Lord, but we have to grow in our understanding of it.

When the centurion whose servant was ill came to Jesus in Matthew, chapter 8, Jesus marveled at his faith. The centurion understood authority. Those over the centurion spoke orders, and he fulfilled them. He spoke to those below him, and they obeyed his orders. He knew that if Jesus, Lord of all, gave the command for his servant to be healed, it would be done. It was simple but amazing.

Most of us have spheres of influence like Johnnie Gray had on the football field and still has on the sidelines. Not all of us realize the great influence and authority God has given us over the situations and conditions in our lives. We often think it's humble to submit to the evils that come into our lives. We recognize that God can bring good out of it, but don't always realize we have the authority to change those situations. We do it with words—not our own words, but the words that Jesus gave us in the Bible. He tells us all His promises are yes and amen (2 Corinthians 1:20). Through His promises, we participate in all that He is (2 Peter 1:4).

We grow in this authority as we exercise it, but we don't earn it. We walk in it simply because we are His. His Spirit dwells in us and works through us. One of the greatest ways for Him to work is through our words. We speak His words to situations and to people. His words administer blessing, healing, and God's best. Read those promises again. Realize they're true, and they belong to you. Use them to bring victory back in your life and in the lives of those around you.

**EXTRA POINT:**

Lord, I believe the promises are for me and that You've given me the authority of Your words. I will look at them anew and begin to walk in them.

*Johnnie Gray, Safety, Inducted into the Packers Hall of Fame 1993*

# Running to Daylight

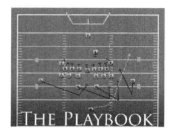

THE PLAYBOOK

**FROM THE PLAYBOOK:**

*Jesus said, "For which of you, intending to build a tower, does not sit down first and count the cost, whether he has enough to finish it?"*

Luke 14:28

**COACH'S CHALLENGE:**

"There's only one way to succeed in anything and that is to give it everything. I do, and I demand that my players do." Vince Lombardi

Coach Lombardi taught that, for the most part, you don't have to decide where you should take the man you block. If that man is trying to go inside, take him there, and the running back goes outside. If he wants to go outside, help him there and the back goes inside. If he seems to have no direction, the Packer player pushes him backwards. That way the running back can head toward daylight through the opening created.[112]

Lombardi was a teacher, a philosopher, and a disciplinarian. He demanded a line of focus and a commitment to the play. With that, games could be won.

Lombardi's intensity endeared him to his players and scared them as well. Henry Jordan summed up the team's sentiments: "Coach Lombardi's very fair. He treats us all like dogs." Willie Davis said they worked hard for Lombardi out of fear and devotion.[113]

The Coach always said God was first. When a player couldn't quite believe Lombardi went to church, Bart Starr replied, "This man *needs* to go to church every single day." [114] Lombardi understood the focus necessary not only for his players but for himself as well. He also understood what motivated his players psychologically. Hornung worked best when Lombardi yelled at him, but shouting embarrassed McGee, so Lombardi gave him a pat on the back instead.[115]

Lombardi always ran to daylight. His legacy was pursuing excellence. His quotes and his winning record have become legendary. Under his direction, the Packers never had a losing season. Their record of 89 wins, 24 losses, and four ties over nine seasons earned them five NFL titles, two of which were Super Bowls I and II.[116]

After Lombardi's death on September 3, 1970, Commissioner Pete Rozelle named the coveted Super Bowl trophy the Lombardi Trophy, perhaps the greatest tribute to this great coach.[117]

I was a college student when I heard Vince Lombardi was ill and dying. Home on summer break, I felt drawn to pray for this man, who to me was an iconic coach in a sport I paid little attention to, and from a place I knew only as the frozen tundra. I grew up on Lake Huron in Michigan and, if anything, considered myself a Lions' fan. About the only football game I paid attention to was the Thanksgiving game each year between the Lions and the Packers. The only Packer fan I knew was the man who owned the gas station in town, and we all thought he was a little crazy. Still, I prayed for Coach Lombardi a great deal. When he died, I thought perhaps I prayed ineffectively, but I wonder to this day if my connection back then prepared me to become a Packer fan and author of *The Cheesehead Devotional.* That time of prayer has always made me feel that in a small way I knew Vince Lombardi.

On that day in September, Coach Lombardi truly ran to daylight. He left a great heritage in football, in leadership, in excellence, and in honoring God. He was disciplined, and he loved his players. Despite his yelling, he was always thankful for the opportunities he received, and he taught his players to be thankful as well.

Do you run to daylight? Do you walk in the light? One aspect of that walk is thankfulness. Without it, we don't progress because we're focused on lack or on failure. When we're thankful, we focus on God, the only one who can bring increase and fruitfulness, the real one who can bring needed change. If focused on Him, He can direct us, and life can be lived to the fullest.

You can fulfill God's best for you.

**EXTRA POINT:**

Lord, help me to run to daylight by honoring You and honoring those around me. I commit to being thankful, which keeps my eyes on You. I'm forever grateful for Your promises and guidance. Help me honor You with a life of excellence.

*Vince Lombardi, Coach, Inducted into the Packers Hall of Fame 1975*

# Sources

1    Bryan Dee, "Antonio Freeman" *ESPN Wisconsin*, pro.wauk-am.tritonflex.com/common/more.php?m=15&r=13&item_id=2941.

2    "Louisiana: Green Bay Packer Fans Celebrate Superbowl Win – 1997" *AP Archive,* July 21, 2015, www.youtube.com/watch?v=qfa_ayknvtg.

3    Reggie White, *In The Trenches*, (Nashville: Thomas Nelson, Inc. Publishers, 1996), 194.

4    History, Hall of Famers, "Reggie White—Class of 2006," *Packers.com.*

5    Hall of Famers, "Reggie White."

6    "Helmet Saves Ray Nitschke as Steel Tower Falls on Him," *Chicago Daily Tribune*, September 2, 1960, archives. chicagotribune.com/1960/09/02/page/43/.

7    Rob Reischel, *100 Things Packers Fans Should Know and Do Before They Die*, (Chicago: Triumph Books, 2010), 40-41.

8    Steve Rose, *Leap of Faith 3: The Packer Hall of Faith,* (Arni Jacobson, "The Last Chapter of #66"), (Neenah: Winners Success Network Publishing 1998), 167.

9    Willie Davis, *Closing the Gap*, (Chicago: Triumph Books 2012), 254.

10   Rose, *Leap of Faith 3*, 164.

11   Reischel, *100 Things*, 41.

12   Jerry Kramer and Dick Schaap, *Instant Replay: The Green Bay Diary of Jerry Kramer*, (New York: Anchor Books, 1968, 2011).

13  Arthur Weinstein, "Five facts about the Packers vs. Cowboys' historic Ice Bowl", *Sporting News*, January 11, 2015, www.sportingnews.com/nfl/news/five-cool-facts-about-the-packers-vs-cowboys-historic-ice-bowl/egkvguzbpeso16x0jrpoa27xt.

14  Steve Sabol and Steve Seidman, *America's Game, The Super Bowl Champions, Super Bowl II, 1967 Green Bay Packers*, (NFL Productions, 2007), DVD.

15  Lori Nickel, "Brett Favre's speech: 'I am so thankful I had an opportunity to play here,'" *Milwaukee Journal Sentinel Online*, July 19, 2015, www.jsonline.com/blogs/sports/317156841.html.

16  Steve Rose, *Leap of Faith: God Must Be a Packer Fan*, (Wautoma: Angel Press of WI, 1996), 142-150.

17  Steve Sabol and David Plaut, *America's Game, The Super Bowl Champions, Super Bowl I, 1966 Green Bay Packers*, (NFL Productions, 2007), DVD.

18  "Memorable Game: 1966 NFL Championship Game," *Golden Football Magazine*, Memorable Game Article, goldenrankings.com/memorablegame1966NFLChampionshipGame.html.

19  Sabol and Plaut, *Super Bowl I*.

20  Sabol and Plaut, *Super Bowl I*.

21  Chris Havel, "Injured trio didn't miss celebration," *Green Bay Press-Gazette*, October 15, 1996, C1.

22  Don Burke, "Nov. 5, 1989: Instant Replay Game," *Milwaukee Journal Sentinel*, Nov. 6, 1989, archives.jsonline.com/sports/packers/183081791.

23  Burke, "Nov. 5, 1989: Instant Replay Game."

24  Eric Gates, "Don 'Majik' Majkowski Highlights, *YouTube*, www.youtube.com/watch?v=ZpIiJ8i5uS0.

25  Reischel, *100 Things*, 82-85.

26   Bud Lea, "Jim Taylor's fearless game stands test of time," *Milwaukee Journal Sentinel Online*, Nov. 8, 2000, JSOnline. com/sports/packers/2454717751.html.

27   Chris Havel, "Beebe speeds into spotlight," *Green Bay Press-Gazette*, Oct. 15, 1996, C1.

28   Pete Dougherty, "Jacke nails 53-yard effort for thrilling overtime win," *Green Bay Press-Gazette*, Oct. 15, 1996, C1.

29   Reischel, *100 Things*, 61-63.

30   Reischel, *100 Things*, 61-63.

31   Emily Kaplan, "The Way of the Wolf," *Sports Illustrated, The College Column MMQB*, Dec. 7, 2016.

32   Reischel, *100 Things*, 61-63.

33   Richard Ryman, "Inside 1265: Packers reflect Mark Murphy," *USA Today Network-Wisconsin*, July 25, 2016, www.packersnews.com/story/sports/nfl/packers/2016/07/22/86570596/.

34   Todd Stelzel, "Who in the heck is Green Bay Packers Clark Hinkle?" *Packers Talk*, www.packerstalk.com/2015/07/25/who-in-the-heck-is-green-bay-packers-clark-hinkle/.

35   Clarke Hinkle's entire Enshrinement Speech-1964, *Enshrinement Quotes*, January 1, 2005, profootballhof.com/news/enshrinement-quotes/.

36   "Packer Back Tosses Shortest Scoring Pass," *Reading Eagle*, November 10, 1942, news.google.com/newspapers?nid=1955&dat=19421110&id.

37   History, Hall of Famers, "Tony Canadeo—Class of 1974," *Packers.com*, packers.com/history/hall-of-famers/canadeo-tony.html.

38   Reischel, *100 Things*, 70-71.

39   Steve Sabol, "Packers vs. Bengals, September 20, 1992", *Packers 10 Greatest Games*, (NFL Productions, 2008) DVD.

40   Sabol, *Greatest Games*.

41    Sabol, *Greatest Games.*

42    Steve Rose, *Leap of Faith*, 85-89.

43    Chuck Carlson, *Tales from the Green Bay Packers Sideline*, (New York: Sports Publishing, 2011), 35.

44    Reischel, *100 Things*, 104-5.

45    "Don Hutson," *Omics International*, research.omicsgroup. org/indes.php/Don_Hutson.

46    Cliff Christl, Packers team historian, "Johnny Blood magical name in Packers history," *Packers.com*, March 26, 2015.

47    Raymond Rivard, "Green Bay Packers: 55 days to football—remembering Johnny Blood McNally," *Lombardi Ave*, lombardiave.com/2015/07/20/green-bay-packers-55-days-to-football-remembering-johnny-blood-mcnally/.

48    Reischel, *100 Things*, 196-197.

49    Reischel, *100 Things*, 12-15.

50    Davis, *Closing the Gap*, 228-233.

51    Davis, *Closing the Gap*, 228-233.

52    Tim Layden, "The man behind the legend: McGee's story goes well beyond SB hangover," *Sports Illustrated*, December 28, 2015, www.si.com/nfl/2015/12/29/max-mcgee-green-bay-packers-super-bowl-I.

53    Layden, "McGee's Story."

54    Layden, "McGee's Story."

55    "About Gilbert," *The Gilbert Brown Foundation*, Gilbertbrownfoundation.org/about.

56    "Clubhouse Live with Gilbert Brown," *Packers News*, August 29, 2016, content.packersnews.com/packersnews/clubhouse/index.php?x=8.

57    "About Gilbert," *The Gilbert Brown Foundation*.

58    "Clubhouse Live with Gilbert Brown," *Packers News*.

59  Bob Wolfey, "Author Sapp explains player Sapp's hit on Packers' Clifton in '02," *Milwaukee Journal Sentinel Online*, July 25, 2012, archive.jsonline.com/blogs/sports/163770296. html.

60  Chris Harry, "Chad Clifton thriving years after Warren Sapp," *SFGate*, February 2, 2011, www.sfgate.com/sports/article/ Chad-Clifton-Thriving-Years-After-Warren-Sapp-2382219. php.

61  Jerry Kramer and Dick Schaap, *Instant Replay, The Green Bay Diary of Jerry Kramer*, 1968, 264.

62  Kramer and Schaap, *Instant Replay*, 265, 266.

63  Davis, *Closing the Gap*, 227-228.

64  Mark Starr, "Starr: Watching NFL Films," *Newsweek*, November 7, 2007, www.newsweek.com/starr-watching-nfl-films-96879.

65  Davis, *Closing the Gap*, 57-61.

66  Reischel, *100 Things*, 92.

67  BentMG, "The First Lambeau Leap," *YouTube*, www.youtube. com/watch?v=MRy-D45Yf_s.

68  Vic Ketchman, "LeRoy Butler toasts new 'Leap Wall' at Lambeau Field," *Packers.com*, Aug. 1, 2014.

69  Rose, *Leap of Faith*, 48.

70  Mike Spofford, "Larry McCarren: The Rock makes no apologies," *Alumni Spotlight*, March 8, 2014, www.packers. com/media-center/videos.

71  "Larry McCarren/On his years in football," *Lombardi Ave*, July 18, 2016, lombardiave.com.

72  Charles Cherney, "Kabeer Gbaja-Biamila sprints down the field for a touchdown," *Chicago Tribune*, www. chicagotribune.com/news/cs-021007gallery_kgb.

73  Martin Hendricks, "Gbaja-Biamila is Packers' all-time sack leader," *Milwaukee Journal Sentinel*, April 27, 2011, archive. jsonline.com/packerinsider/120709899.html.

74  Mike Miller, "Member Spotlight: Kabeer and Eileen Gbaja-Biamila, former Muslim and NFL player is now a Christian financial adviser," *Samaritan Ministries*, April 2001, Samaritanministries.org/blog/member-spotlight-kabeer-and-eileen-gbaja-biamila.

75  Rose, *Leap of Faith 3*, 40.

76  Pete Dougherty, "Injury shelves Brooks for year," *Green Bay Press Gazette*, Oct. 15, 1996, C3.

77  Rose, *Leap of Faith 2: God Loves Packer Fans*, (Madison:Prairie Oak Press, 1997), 35-43.

78  Carlson, *Packers Sideline*, 77-84.

79  Peter Jackal, "Winters still going strong," *Journal Times*, December 5, 2002, journaltimes.com/sports/winters-still-going-strong/article_d040856d-a436-5638-9779-02dbce70a6e0.html.

80  Jose E. Garcia, "Fred Carr devoted to friends, family, and work," *The Arizona Republic*, August 6, 2010, archive. azcentral.com/sports/preps/articles/20100806.

81  Alpha Dragon, Ahman Green Highlights, *YouTube*, September 16, 2014, youtube.com/watch?v-UnBYN_1rA8c&t=10s.

82  Martin Hendricks, "Ahman Green powered his way into Packer's record book," *Milwaukee Journal Sentinel*, August 18, 2011, archive.jsonline.com.

83  Hendricks, "Ahman Green."

84  Tom Fanning, "Green Preparing For Next Chapter," *Packers. com*, March 20, 2010.

85  Johnny Holland, *Life Stories*, TheGoal.com/players/football/holland_johnny/holland_johnny.html.

86 Tsimosjones58, "Hendo layin' the leather to Lewis," *YouTube*, May 2, 2013, youtube.com/watch?v=6gpKrCZWS2A.

87 Paul Imig, "Retired Henderson remains loyal to Packers," *Fox Sports Wisconsin*, April 2, 2013.

88 NFL, "Aaron Rodgers' Improbable Game Winning Hail Mary Pass! Ultimate Highlight NFL Films," *YouTube*, December 4, 2015, youtube.com/watch?v=Q8QBaziudTo.

89 Snow Bowl (1985), *Wikipedia*, https://en.wikipedia.org/w/index.php?title=Snow_Bowl(1985)&oldid=719131878.

90 Keith Yowell, "1985: Packers Shut Out Bucs in 'Snow Bowl,'" *Today in Pro Football History*, December 1, 2015, fs64sports.blogspot.com/2015/12/1985-packers-shut-out-buccaneers-in.html.

91 UPI, "Packers 21, Bucs 0, Snow 16," *The New York Times*, December 2, 1985.

92 Davis, *Closing the Gap*, 241.

93 Davis, *Closing the Gap*, 240-242.

94 Richard Goldstein, "Elijah Pitts, 60, Star Back for Storied Packers," *The New York Times*, July 11, 1998.

95 Martin Hendricks, "Elijah Pitts a versatile player," *Packer Plus*, October 24, 2012.

96 Hendricks, "Pitts versatile player."

97 Gary D'Amato, "Adderley reflects on time with Packers," *Milwaukee Journal Sentinel*, Nov. 22, 2012.

98 Green Bay Press Gazette, "Former Packers player Herb Adderley," *YouTube*, November 30, 2012, www.youtube.com/watch?v=xS4ZKESrBII.

99 Jimmy the Jet, "Donald Driver's one-handed catch against the St. Louis Rams," *YouTube*, September 28, 2009, www.youtube.com/watch?v=NkMmFFqK6yo.

100  Basaraski Productions, "Donald Driver Tribute/Career Highlights," *YouTube*, April 18, 2015, www.youtube.com/watch?v=Zu5LgpmdcjQ#+.

101  Jimmy the Jet, "Driver's one-handed catch."

102  Bill Pennington, "Willie Wood Made the Most Memorable Play of Super Bowl 1. He Has No Recollection," *New York Times*, February 4, 2016, nyti.ms/20bpg2v.

103  Pennington, "Wood Memorable Play."

104  Reischel, *100 Things*, 63-66.

105  Scott Schalin, "The Mad Ride of Packers Hall of Famer Lionel Aldridge," *Lombardi Ave*, June 14, 2012, packershalloffame.com/players/lionel-aldridge/.

106  Reischel, *100 Things*, 53-56.

107  "Lombardi and The Sweep," Manufacturing Strategy, Vince Lombardi & The Power Sweep, *Strategos*, April, 2014, www.strategosinc.com/lombardi.htm.

108  Ed Gruver, "The Lombardi Sweep," *The Coffin Corner: Vol. 19, No. 5* (1997), www.profootballresearchers.org/archives/Website_Files/Coffin_Corner/19-05-712.pdf.

109  Carlson, *Packers Sideline*, 114-119.

110  Jersey Al Bracco, "Green Bay Packers Greatest Undrafted Free Agent Finds," *All Green Bay Packers*, May 5, 2010, allgbp.com/2010/05/05/green-bay-packers-greatest-undrafted-free-agent-finds/.

111  Jerry Crowe, "Johnny Gray is a stickler for NFL professionalism," *Los Angeles Times*, October 3, 2010, articles.latimes.com/2010/oct/03/sports/la-sp-crowe-20101004.

112  Kramer and Schaap, *Instant Replay*, 89.

113  Davis, *Closing the Gap*, 82.

114  Sabol, *Super Bowl I*.

[115] Pat Williams, *Vince Lombardi on Leadership: Life Lessons from a Five-Time NFL Championship Coach*, (Charleston: Advantage Media Group), 2015.

[116] Bob Fox, "Green Bay Packers: Vince Lombardi Was the Very Best in His Dual Roles as Head Coach and General Manager," *Green Bay Bob Fox*, June 3, 2016, greenbaybobfox. wordpress.com/2016/06/03/green-bay-packers-vince-lombardi-was-the-very-best-in-his-dual-roles-as-head-coach-and-general-manager/.

[117] History, Hall of Famers, "Vince Lombardi – Class of 1971," *Packers.com*, www.packers.com/history/hall-of-famers/lombardi-vince.html.

**Sources of Vince Lombardi Quotes:**

Goodreads.com

BrainyQuote.com

Successories.com

Laughteronlineuniversity.com

Wow4u.com

Motivational.com

Insidethehuddle.tv

Ranker.com

Quotesigma.com

*Closing the Gap*, Willie Davis

*Instant Replay*, Jerry Kramer and Dick Schaap

Lambeau Field Atrium

Packers Hall of Fame

Made in the USA
Middletown, DE
18 September 2018